How to Live
with
Other
People's
Children

ALSO BY JUNE AND WILLIAM NOBLE
The Custody Trap

HOW TO LIVE WITH OTHER PEOPLE'S CHILDREN

June and William Noble

HAWTHORN BOOKS, INC.
Publishers / NEW YORK
A Howard & Wyndham Company

For our children
and especially
for Leigh Ruth

HOW TO LIVE WITH OTHER PEOPLE'S CHILDREN

Copyright © 1977 by June and William Noble. Copyright under International and Pan-American Copyright Conventions. All rights reserved, including the right to reproduce this book or portions thereof in any form, except for the inclusion of brief quotations in a review. All inquiries should be addressed to Hawthorn Books, Inc., 260 Madison Avenue, New York, New York 10016. This book was manufactured in the United States of America and published simultaneously in Canada by Prentice-Hall of Canada, Limited, 1870 Birchmount Road, Scarborough, Ontario.

Library of Congress Catalog Card Number: 76-53390
ISBN: 0-8015-3862-9
3 4 5 6 7 8 9 10

Contents

Acknowledgments

We want to express our appreciation to the many people who helped us while we researched this book. We are particularly indebted to the professionals who gave their time and observations.

—Brandon Adams, M.D., Nyssa, Oregon

—Vera Bangsberg, juvenile officer, Police Department, Oakland, California

—Michael Beausang, Esq., attorney, King of Prussia, Pennsylvania

—Dr. Willem Bosma, psychiatrist, Baltimore, Maryland

—Jean Chastain, child psychologist, Berkeley, California

—Dr. Margaret Doren, psychologist, Saint Paul, Minnesota

—William Dowdell, psychologist, Middlebury, Vermont

—Natalie Duany, MSW, Vergennes, Vermont

—Joanne Frankel, MSW, marriage and family counselor, Portland, Oregon

—Murray Gegner, MSW, marriage and family counselor, Ventnor, New Jersey

—Dr. Hans Huessey, psychiatrist, Burlington, Vermont

—Dr. Edna Kamis, psychologist, Philadelphia, Pennsylvania

—Dr. Dana Lehman-Olson, psychologist, Burnsville, Minnesota

—Dr. Gordon Livingston, psychiatrist, Columbia, Maryland

—Dr. Gary Margolis, psychologist, Middlebury, Vermont

—Dr. Dwight Mowry, psychologist, Payette, Idaho

—Frankie Mae Paulson, psychologist, Minneapolis, Minnesota

—William Riggs, Esq., attorney, Portland, Oregon

—Dr. Frank Strange, psychologist, Portland, Oregon

—Dr. Robert Templeton, psychologist, Middlebury, Vermont

And to the special friends who became directly involved with our work: Nancy Means Wright, Helga Brogger, Elizabeth Kolowrat, Ray and Grace Wojda, Barbara Kingsley, Dona and David Hoard, Linda Odum-Duncan, Anke Immink, Dianne Brogger.

Introduction

This book had its origin in another—a chapter from a work on remarriage. Our editor, Elizabeth Backman, must be credited for seeing that chapter expanded into a larger work and for encouraging us to translate our stepfamily experiences into workable solutions for questions that are commonly asked and problems that are universal.

For nine years we have both been involved with each other's children, first in a living-together arrangement and then within a marriage. Our mistakes and misjudgments were many, our expectations were frequently unrealistic, our successes moderate. We have learned much from interviewing other couples and professionals, fortunately some of it not too late to use even now, although our children are teen-aged and beyond. It would have helped us a lot, though, if we had known back then what step relationships could or should be and had some cautionary professional advice about what to do.

We arranged taped interviews with stepparents and stepchildren coast to coast, went into their homes, prompted them with questions, and listened to their stories. Some of our chosen stepparents were behavioral professionals—psychologists, psychiatrists, sociologists—because we were looking for positive approaches that might be developed from people who had lived through the step situation on two dimensions, as advice givers and as participants. In addition, we consulted with other professionals, and their evaluations also provided the necessary springboard for learning how to live successfully with other people's children.

But by far the bulk of those we spoke with were nonprofessionals—men, women, and children who were willing to share their experiences for nothing more than a promise of anonymity. When we began each interview by noting that we, too, were stepparents, there was an immediate bonding. "Fellow sufferers!" said one stepfather. "Have I got some questions for *you*," responded a young stepmother. For the truth is that stepparenting is an experience that takes on added meaning when it can be shared.

And sharing experiences is one way to gain perspective and understanding. We are familiar with the fairy tales that involve a wicked stepmother—Hansel and Gretel, Snow White, Cinderella—and we may scoff at their application in our modern world. Yet for little children with a big imagination, the dark side of stepparenting can seem all too real. A stepmother from Cleveland described her first meeting with her two stepsons. "My husband and I had been married for only a month, and I had never met his sons. They lived in Chicago, and their mother reluctantly agreed to let them fly East for their two-week visit. But from the moment they walked off the plane, they tried to avoid me, actually hiding behind their father when I reached out to touch them, mumbling answers when I tried to talk to them. It wasn't until the day they were to return that my husband got to the bottom of it. Two days before their visit their mother had taken them to see the movie *Cinderella*!"

In this sense the burdens of stepparenting have stayed constant. The stepparent is still the outsider, still an easy target for scorn, the uncertain figure in the family. There is still a general expectation for a family adult to assume the job of parent even though there may be no biological tie with the family. Are our concepts of these roles so fixed that some parental relationship *must* develop? Can't something less formal but just as meaningful work out?

It is simply asking too much for a stepparent—who begins as a rank outsider—to materialize as a parent without much time and travail. Our interviews pointed to years of effort before such strong kinship was established, and in most cases the relationships never reached this level. Yet many adults, in the beginning, pictured themselves in the parental role, rarely questioning why they should have such aspirations, building air castles of a new family. They found it difficult to grasp that living with other people's children means different rules, different expectations, different solutions.

Different, however, need not mean less satisfying. It's all in how we see ourselves and in how much effort we intend to expend in order to make our relationships work. The adult who believes it is necessary to become an instant parent is bound to be disappointed. The adult who strives for an easy familiarity and nothing more will see the fruits returned in time.

For those of us who have lived with other people's children, the magic lies not in assuming a role but in creating an honest relationship which we can nurture. This book, we hope, will help you reach that goal.

1
GETTING READY

Preparing for Stepchildren

If there is one commandment in stepfamily relationships, it is that you talk out your expectations as early as possible. Otherwise you will all be jolted when you find out that the children don't behave in the ways you anticipated. Or you will bluntly discover that your mate is totally at odds with the way you think the children should be raised.

The most crucial expectation to be worked out is the one dealing with discipline, and it should be discussed early. One stepfather who is also a psychologist said, "While we were living together before we made the marriage commitment, we usually discussed our expectations late at night, after the children had gone to bed. We did it in the context of questions:

- What is it that you do or don't like about spanking?
- What other forms of discipline are you for or against?
- Do you mind when they talk back?
- How do you react to hurtful and cutting remarks?
- How do you react to manipulation?

It isn't really essential that you both have an identical approach to each of these items, but it is important that each of you *knows* how the other feels and will react. Then, if one person's reaction is particularly offensive, it can be explored and some accommodation reached. Put another way, ideally, there should be few, if any, surprises about how either of you feels or what either of you says by the time the children begin to live with you.

Part of any preparation for stepchildren is to understand the limitations of being a stepparent. You have no biological ties to the children; you are there solely because you happen to marry or be living with their parent. Any respect, any deference you get will probably have to be earned; nothing comes to you by virtue of position within the family. In many ways you will have to prove yourself to become accepted.

There are people, however, who try to fool themselves into thinking that stepparenthood can be something more. "Being a stepparent is quite similar to being an adoptive parent," says psychiatrist Gordon Livingston. "People go into it with a whole set of fantasies, believing it's a natural thing, saying to themselves, 'I'm a loving person, and it's just like having my own kid.' Suddenly it turns out not to be." Unless he's a baby, a stepchild is like an older child you have adopted. He will have a well-formed personality by the time you meet him, and it's inevitable that clashes will develop over your expectations about behavior, manners, attitudes, and so forth. "Then you feel doubly betrayed," Livingston points out. Not only does the child make you realize you have no biological ties, but also all the loving you planned to give won't make the difference. "There is something about the biological tie that has a certain importance," Livingston concludes, "and knowing one is genetically connected to a child is never quite made up for in our dealings with stepchildren."

This, however, has nothing to do with a stepparent's rights, and both natural parents as well as their children should be aware of this. Take the family car, for instance. If an adult is paying the insurance, then he or she should have a say in how the car is used, where it is used, and when. "Stepparents should have some rights about things that directly affect them," says psychologist Dana Lehman-Olson. "It's really unfair to them if their needs aren't taken into account if their stepchildren's actions directly affect them." In preparing yourself for the children it would be wise to talk about those areas where their actions will have an effect on you, your pocketbook, your reputation, your tranquility.

"What I encourage parents to do," continues Dana Lehman-Olson, "is to sort out where the consequences of children's actions bear on them directly and where they are only peripheral. Many times parents set arbitrary rules of behavior that stem from emotional reactions, so I urge them to shift to the children as much of the responsibility as they can. And as the children get older, they should share more and more of the responsibility for such things as paying for their own car insurance, making their own car payments, paying for their own telephone, smoking pot away from the house. And I believe parents should begin to minimize to themselves the consequences of those things over which they have granted the children so much control."

However, before you shuck off certain responsibilities to your mate's children, you should work it out with him. It may seem to be a perfectly logical thing to insist that no pot smoking be allowed in the house because you could be held accountable. But your mate may feel otherwise and may take offense at your assuming to make rules for his or her child. That's why it's so important to deal with your expectations ahead of time, to agree at least on certain principles. It's quite common for natural parents to resent intrusions by stepparents, but when the parent denies reasonable authority to his mate, the entire relationship is bound to suffer. "You find stepparents just resenting the hell out of parents when they do that," says psychologist Dwight Mowry. "It's like, 'When we married, it was my understanding that we were going to be equals, and now you're telling me we're not, that ultimately you have the responsibility for the kids and I don't.' That makes the mate an outsider pretty quickly in some emotional ways and certainly in some behavioral ways."

How have some parents' mates prepared for the children?

Some have sought professional help to learn about the problems within the new household. Clara realized quickly that there were some deep problems between her two young stepsons-to-be. Their mother had died three years before, and the boys were constantly at each other's throats. For a year or more their father had been taking them to see a child psychologist, so Clara decided to talk with him too. "He told me that a lot of the hostility went back to the former marriage, where the mother favored the younger boy. Anything that was wrong around the house, the older boy got blamed, even if the younger one had done it. The mother was really cruel to him. The younger boy used to manipulate his older brother and really ran the house before the mother died. He carried this same behavior over to his relationship with the housekeeper and father." The child psychologist advised Clara not to let the manipulation continue. "I've told the older boy to think about what he's saying, what he's trying to do. Is he just teasing?" Has it worked? "The boys fight much more rarely now."

Some have allowed the natural parent to observe them with the children over a period of time. Benjamin retained custody of his two girls when his marriage broke up. Three years later he met Susan and decided he wanted to marry her—but not before he could judge what kind of relationship she could have with his children. "I observed Susan for a considerable period of time, both with my children and with her children. I felt very comfortable with the way she would handle a crisis, and the way she handled the parent role." Has it worked? "Everything since then has confirmed what my observations showed."

Some haven't tried to short-cut their discussions about expectations. Both Mary and Steve had been married before, and between them they had eight children. Though they knew quickly after meeting that they wanted to live with each other, they deliberately dampened their impatience. "It was probably an entire year before Steve moved in and another few months before we were married," Mary said. "We spent hours and hours—drinking gallons and gallons of tea—as we talked everything out. We went into what our roles would be, how much of a father he would be to my kids, how much of a mother I would be to his, whether we would take the other parent's place. We decided to try and be good people, to build relationships with each child, and that that was more important than having a kid call you mom or dad." Has it worked? "I feel that our year of talking things out is an important part of what we have today."

Some have been ready to change their habits for a while. Nancy is a social worker whose first marriage ended without children. Before she married her second husband, she weighed the fact that he had custody of his two little boys, aged two and three. So she gave up her job for a while. "I spent time at home with the boys when they first came with us, the same as I would do if I had my own children that age. After a while, when they were used to me and the house, I went back to work. I love children, but I also love working. But the children know that if for some reason they had really needed me, I'd have stayed home longer." Has it worked? "We have our own child, I stayed home for a year and a half, and as far as I'm concerned there's no difference between them. They seem to feel the same."

Most professionals are adamant about the dangers of rushing into a new marriage and not taking the time to get yourself ready for the children. Call it a testing period if you wish, but you should sort out your feelings and weigh your reactions under a variety of circumstances. You should determine when you will be stepping on your mate's toes in questions of discipline, authority, money, relations with the other natural parent, modesty within the home, social habits. It takes time to work these through, and it's best done before the final commitment.

One social worker who is a stepparent and also the stepdaughter of another told us, "If there's any way to do it, prolong your experience with the children before you marry so you can get an idea of what the problems are and whether you're going to be able to work them out. While it isn't exactly the same thing as having the children with you when you're married, at least you get ideas about what kinds of things bother you about them and whether or not your new mate is going to allow you to be bothered."

Telling the Children About the New Marriage

Children deserve to have the new marriage event handled as you would a dog with pups—with care and great respect.

We discovered two things that stepchildren remember vividly. First, that time when their parents split, that moment when their old lives came apart. They can even recall what the weather was like or what they were wearing.

A second thing they remember, with varying degrees of anger, anguish, uncertainty, or happiness, is when they found out their parent was going to get married again. Many times, we learned, preparing children for the new marriage wasn't handled very well. At least this is the way the children felt, and it was this unfortunate circumstance that was carried, like unwanted baggage, into the shared home.

One stepmother in the five years since her wedding has had some long soul-searching conversations with her stepchildren, a boy now fifteen and a girl now twelve. Before the marriage she had never considered them an integral part of her future life. They lived with their mother and would be weekend and vacation visitors. Yet, even as visitors, they did become an important part—if not always a welcome part—of her life, and the three of them have talked out events that led up to that momentous day when their father remarried and irrevocably cut off their wishful hope that he belonged first and foremost to them.

The stepmother recalled, "The surprising thing I found out from them—and they definitely are not making this up—is that they were never told about their father's remarriage until after it took place. I know that this perception is not accurate because I had had conversations with them about our forthcoming wedding. They had frequently visited this house, which they assumed was mine, although in fact their dad and I were sharing it. The interesting thing is that whatever we told them didn't penetrate. And the way they remember it, which is the important thing, is that they were *not* told. They think that they remember I was just a friend, someone their dad liked, but really we were just buddies. I can understand this on the part of my stepdaughter, who suddenly was faced with the reality that her father had taken up with this new woman when surely she should have been all he needed. It was something like, 'Why do you need her when you've got me?' I suppose her attitude influenced the boy's."

But there was more than an attitude at work here. Both this stepmother and her husband were very careful during the period when they were living together not to let it become apparent to the kids. They were afraid of the consequences to his pending divorce and afraid that the children's mother could pull the chain on visitation or change the divorce grounds to adultery. Yet this was still no good reason for not including the children in the marriage plans, and now both the stepmother and father regret it. She said, "If we had it to do over again, I think I would have found a way to be more open with the kids. We should have been more sensitive to what they were hearing. We didn't realize how little they *did* hear about our getting married. If we could do the wedding a second time, they would be part of the ceremony. They knew it was going to happen—even if they deny it—but we didn't ask them to attend."

Not being involved in this most important part of a parent's life makes a child feel unimportant—even second-rate. It's almost embarrassing when they realize how little they count. One bright college girl recalls, "I knew my father had a new love interest, although being in love and deciding to get married are quite different things. My sister was living with him at the time, and as I walked into the junior high that day, she came up to me and said, 'Can you keep a secret?' I said, 'Sure.' She said, 'Dad's going to get married. He told me but asked me not to tell anyone.' I said something like, Gee, that's great. I like her kids!' And I did. I thought it would be fun living with them. Well, a couple of days later my father called me and said, 'I've a surprise to tell you.' I remember saying nothing, just waiting. He said, 'I want to tell you the good news. I'm getting married.' I was appropriately surprised, because of course I could keep a secret. What I felt was different. I guess I felt, 'Well, big deal.' I don't think news like that ought to be parceled out to one child at a time. Maybe he was just trying to punish me a little bit or showing me that my sister was more a part of his life because I was living with my mother. What's the outcome? Well, I don't think I'd go to him with any problems—and certainly not with any secrets."

Another stepdaughter recalls, "One day we were driving in the car with my mother, and she asked how would we like to have a father? We knew who he was, but we were all shocked. And that's all we learned about our future life until the wedding. I liked the idea of a stepfather, I liked the thought of it because I thought in terms of someone to go fishing with, and my brother thought in terms of someone to play baseball with. Until the wedding we didn't find out he didn't fish or play ball."

A stepson recalls, "I heard them talking over the back fence to our next-door neighbor. I eased myself down in the side yard and heard them go over all their marriage plans. My mother had never said anything to me or his kids before this, so I told his kids. They were as surprised as I was and wondered why our parents hadn't come to us first. I got the feeling my mother didn't consider me worthwhile enough to consult, and I was right."

Of course there are many kids who don't find out about the future marriage in this manner, just as there are many kids who know, through the vibrations, that a marriage is coming up and who even promote it. One good step relationship began in this way.

The children's mother told us, "It's hard to keep up with our kids. They're super smart, and even though their stepfather and I met at a Mensa meeting, they can run circles around us. I'm sure that not only mine but other gifted children are equally perceptive. They were eleven, nine, and seven when we started dating, and I didn't think it appeared all that serious. Because I had the kids at home alone, I made a lot of home-cooked meals, and we dated in our apartment. I was seeing other men at the time, and Larry and I had a nice but tentative relationship. I was in the kitchen stirring the pot when to my horror I overheard one childish voice say, 'Would you like to be our daddy?' I thought, 'Oh, my god,' but I felt there wasn't much I could do but pretend I hadn't heard anything and just continue cooking, which I did. Over the next three months the children continued to show enthusiasm for Larry, and it became more and more reciprocated. He had no children of his own, so they began to figure he belonged to them. We just had to finally say, 'Okay, we're going to get married.' So we told them, and all of a sudden he had three children climbing all over him, saying 'Daddy, daddy!' He hugged them, then in mock seriousness said, 'Could we wait for the ceremony?' Of course they couldn't. He was already theirs, and they stood up at the marriage ceremony as well, an early Christmas package to the new groom."

The children were so ready for this marriage that even during preparations they went to school and announced that their names had been changed. Their mother respected their eagerness and talked privately to the teachers. "I told them, 'Their hearts are set on this, finally having a father, and I don't care what you put on the school records! They're going to be adopted anyway, but for now would you be willing to call them by the name they prefer?' The teachers all agreed, and the kids started on a good step relationship that seven years later is even better.

Not preparing children for the fact that a most important person is coming into your life can have repercussions for years. Sometimes an almost unconscious embarrassment about the remarriage can keep a parent silent on the matter. Sometimes it's just a question of thoughtlessness. A new stepparent can really feel left out if his or her status is not enhanced and clarified by the natural parent's announcement. The children's reaction can range from indifference to overt hostility.

One father is still pondering why his daughter wants to have nothing to do with his new wife. They've been married for three years, and the situation has still not softened. There's little doubt that he bungled it before the ceremony. Tom, a Roman Catholic who had been married to a staunch churchwoman, had a couple of sons and two teen-age daughters at the time of his serious involvement with Terry. But Terry was someone he never talked about. He would visit his children in their home, take the girls shopping or out for lunch, take the boys to ball games—but never out with Terry. Terry's status was never clear. The children had been indoctrinated by their religious training both from their mother and from the church to view marriage in absolute and indissoluble terms. Tom made no move to contradict this by talking about his own exception.

Terry and Tom were married in a clerk's office, and it was wholly their affair. No children attended, and the announcement was just as casual. The logical extension of this took root in daughter Diane's mind that if this marriage is not worth discussing and celebrating, then what's so special about this woman? Tom also feels that Diane regards Terry as the cause of the first marriage's breakup, a suspicion without foundation but one that he's never disabused her of. To this day Diane refuses to refer to Terry as a stepmother. Tom related, "Once I said to her, 'Do you think you'd like to get your stepmother something for her birthday?' and she snapped back, 'I have no stepmother.' I said, 'Don't be ridiculous. Of course you have a stepmother. It's Terry, and she's married to me, your father.' She said 'She's not my stepmother.' I said, 'Of course she is.' She had no more to say."

Diane is determined to treat Terry as a nonperson. One Saturday her father picked her up to take her to his home, and on the way Diane asked to stop for a hamburger. When they arrived at Terry and Tom's house, a special lunch was on the table, Diane's favorite cold cuts and salads. She looked at the table and said offhandedly, "I've already eaten, thanks."

Probably the situation won't improve, but even at this late date Tom might be able to rectify some of his missteps by honest words. Diane's conception of who Terry was and is can only be altered by Tom owning up to his past and to his mistakes while he started down the road to his remarriage. It could work out, because Diane is smart. For her stepmother's sake, anyway, Diane ought to be shown that her anger is directed at the wrong person. It really belongs on Tom's back if in fact it belongs anywhere.

Gail Stark wrote a first-person account of the process of preparing for her own remarriage.* Both she and her new husband had young children from a previous marriage, seven in all. Through the period of getting to know each other, the children became more and more involved. Family get-togethers such as picnics and excursions helped to smooth the transition from "just friends" to friends and relations. The six months of getting to know one another, she tells, witnessed open hostility at the start and an eagerness to share house and board at the end. It was the kids who suggested the two parents get married, once again sensing the vibes around them and welcoming the possibility of something permanent. Ms. Stark said she realized it was the gradual growth of intimacy among the children as well as among the parents that contributed to the good start in their marriage. She is convinced that children have a right to know ahead of time about the profound changes that come with remarriage. In this instance plans for a new house were discussed as well as plans for the wedding itself. So the wedding ceremony was not just the icing on the cake or a program for adults only.

A wedding may be just a wedding to us, but to kids it's more than flowers, candles, toasts, and vows. To them it means changed living arrangements, perhaps moving away, giving up rights, testing behavior, and sharing with people not their own.

Adjusting the Children to Living with You

"I thought we were getting along great, and we really liked each other. Then she started living with us," said a Berkeley, California, stepmother.

What went wrong with the "great" relationship? What happened

*Parents Magazine, May 1971, p. 45.

between the time of the adults' courtship, when the little girl asked if she could call her "mommy," and the marriage, when the little girl said venomously, "My daddy and I don't like the way you cook. My grandma fixes it better."

The reasons, as in the breakdown of many friendships, are complicated. Yet this stepmother seemed to agree with other parents' mates that the living situation could have been improved if a little more thought had been given to preparing the child to live with them.

Among the suggestions that stepparents and professionals agree are helpful when bringing an already formed young person into your life are these:

- It is necessary to know what kind of person you are—demanding? easygoing? meticulous? disorganized?
- It is important to project your true personality to the child; you must allow her to see the real you before you share a full-time relationship.
- You must help the child reveal to you what she expects from you.
- You should be able to project the security of your future homelife and how you hope to achieve it.
- You should try to clear away misconceptions that developed during the courtship.
- You must involve the children in any planning that will affect them.
- You should guarantee to the child respect for her possessions, attachments, and involvements.

Some parents' mates have the advantage of being able, over a long period of time, gently to condition the children for their eventual living together. Others become custodial stepparents almost overnight, and while this is far from easy, with open communication it can still work out. Most often the communication becomes a monologue, but even that is better than not revealing who you are, what you expect, and what you have to offer.

Involving the children in plans for the future can include finding a new house. One Chicago stepmother who married a widower with two boys decided she wanted to start fresh in a home of her own. But

she was sensitive enough to talk to the boys about the new neighborhood and discovered that they didn't mind moving to a better neighborhood but wanted to stay in the same school. With these parameters they picked out a house, brought the boys around to choose
their rooms and color scheme, and involved them in planning whose
furniture would go where. It seems like a small gesture, but it was
part of her effort to make the boys feel secure with her.

She took further steps to let them know what sort of a stepmother
she might be. During the three months before the wedding she made
a point of sharing mealtimes and afternoons with them. She said,
"The boys frequently came to my house for dinner, and we did family things together, like going to the shopping center, picnics, sailing.
But I also got in the habit, since my work schedule permitted, of going over to their home after I got off from work and telling the
housekeeper she could take off early. I'd fix dinner, take them to the
doctor, the dentist, or the library. That sort of thing."

But it took a crisis to let the thirteen-year-old boy know what he
could expect from his future stepmother. It was six weeks before the
wedding when the boy was accused of serious vandalism by a couple
of neighbors. "I knew it wasn't factual," she recalled. "On the dates
that the events occurred, the boy was with me, not in the neighborhood at the time. At first I couldn't figure out what was going on.
But because of my background in juvenile justice work I knew it had
to be a child of one of the people reporting this to the police, because
only he had described our boy as being the one doing this. It was a
difficult thing to handle, and I took it on myself to explain to him
how serious it was and the lengths he would have to go to clear his
name. We gave him the difficult choice of being completely super-
vised after school every day so some adult could account for his time
or going to his uncle's farm in the country. He decided to go away,
so his father took him out of school early. No one knew that he had
left the neighborhood. The vandalism continued, and the neighbors
came down to accuse him. I immediately called his uncle's house to
make arrangements for the police to go out and verify that he was
there. Although he's never verbalized his feelings about what I did to
help him, I felt good about it, and I think he began to see my
strengths and my ability to handle certain situations. It showed that I
knew what to do, how to take care of it, that I flat out believed my
stepson and was going to do everything I could to prove him inno-

cent. I'm glad to say that eventually the real vandal was caught by his own father after doing eight hundred dollars worth of damage."

Frequently the honeymoon between stepparent and child comes before they start living together, as was the case of the Berkeley stepmother whose stepdaughter turned on her after the wedding. "When I first met my stepdaughter, she was an adorable four-year-old. Here I was, a kindergarten teacher, and I knew every game little girls liked to play. When I came to her house I'd give her full attention, play with her, hug her, give her treats. Before her father and I even talked about marriage she asked when she could call me 'mommy,' and I was so flattered I let her call me that right away. The shocker came when we moved in together, and I had to become the disciplinarian instead of the nice, playful kindergarten teacher with a bag of tricks up her sleeve. I was no longer the person who came around and played but the person who said, 'It's time to take your bath,' or 'It's time to go to bed.' Suddenly she seemed to react as if she didn't need this. She would show it in many ways, like pulling her hand out of mine when we crossed streets and running to her daddy."

It's evident to this stepmother as she recounted those events of ten years before that she had done little to prepare the child for the realities of life ever after with her. It could not continue to be ice cream and cake, games and songs. It had to include 'Go to bed, get your bath, take my hand,' and somehow this transition should have been started before the wedding. Talking to the little girl would not have been enough, for as many stepparents have learned, what is told and what is digested or perceived are often unrelated. But beyond this error of omission, the stepmother missed a few other things. She had not dispassionately examined the events and forces beyond her own involvement that were working on this child. She did not recognize the child's cupidity and so wasn't ready to deal with it. If she hadn't been so anxious for the marriage, so flattered to be "liked," she might have done some soul-searching and started out on a more realistic basis. Who wouldn't like a sugar and spice lady who knocked herself out? What she had also put out of her head is that little children frequently "like" someone only for self-serving reasons, and this was the flimsiest emotion possible on which to launch a decade or more of togetherness.

Some parents' mates, through sheer egocentricity or because of a lack of parenting experience, are brutally ignorant of just what the children may expect from them. One stepfather whose relationship with the children had, from their point of view, been a disaster, said, "I don't recall our sitting down before we were married and talking about what we expected from each other or what I thought or the kids thought each of us would be like. But if we had talked, it wouldn't have helped much. I'm the way I am, and I don't think that would change. I was always on the road during the week, and on the weekends I'd tell them to do this or do that, and my wife would say, 'You don't know what they've been doing all week, so you shouldn't try to take over everything on the weekend.' Well, I'm a takeover person. I didn't like their conduct when I came home, for instance. You would think that if you've been away working all week, that when you come home on the weekends it would be a good relationship, not that you had to jump in there and correct them all the time."

His stepdaughter relates, "We didn't know what he was like until the wedding. I thought a stepfather would be something great, someone who took an interest in you and listened to you. He never praised us, just punished us. It wasn't until I grew up that I found out his own father beat him every night, that he was afraid to express any warm feelings that might appear to make him less macho. If we had known more about him and what life had been like for him as a kid, if he had talked more about things like that, it would have helped us to understand him. We weren't bad kids, but we sure wanted to get back at him all the time, instead of cooperating. Even if my mother had told us more about him—but there wasn't that kind of talk in our house."

One stepmother from Minneapolis got to know her future stepson over a three-year period and feels that this contributed markedly toward their good kinship. Getting to know one another involved sleeping at the future stepmother's house or spending a weekend with her and his future stepgrandparents. Tammy is Chinese, and the respect for one another's person is common to her culture. Although the stepson was half Caucasian, his father was Chinese, so the boy fitted well into the Chinese home environment. Tammy used to have the boy visit her at least two weekends a month, and on Sundays the three of them would go hunting and fishing. Their love of the outdoors provided a good meeting place to share stories, feelings, and expectations. "His father worked on Saturdays, so that day would be totally mine with the boy or with him and my parents. He saw me in my natural home atmosphere and how I respected and loved my parents."

Being a part of this let the boy know subtly that he would be expected to act the same way. His mother was glad to give him up, and since she had abused him from babyhood, he was glad to turn to a loving family. Surely if Tammy had come on the scene quickly, he might have been fearful and defensive, not knowing what to expect from this new lady. But the time they spent living together on camping expeditions and at her parents' home reassured him that with this mother there would be love in place of abuse.

But few parents' mates have the benefit of long acquaintanceship to ready the children for living with them. Sometimes living arrangements or marriages happen almost overnight; sometimes a visiting stepchild suddenly becomes a permanent or semipermanent resident in the household. When this happens, it's vital that there be immediate communication between the adults and each child. One psychologist suggests having a family gathering before moving-in time—or immediately afterward if that's more practical. At this time you pledge to the child, in whatever way seems most natural and most comfortable, that the attachments and the involvements the young person has already formed will not be threatened. If the person is into hard rock or imbecilic television shows, for instance, you won't demand that because he's in your house, he's to forgo all of that. You might talk about earphones or a special room so you won't be driven up the wall. You should let the child know that the relationship between her and your mate is theirs alone—you won't insist on being a part of it. You may have to grit your teeth a bit to say this, but if you can, you can be sure the child won't feel unduly threatened when you begin to make some demands of your own.

The dialogue between one stepmother, her mate, and his fifteen-year-old son, who decided to move in with them, lasted over a period of a week. "We went over the chores that had to be done, we talked allowances, telephone manners, the hours when it was a must that the telephone be free for our calls, and we had some morality lectures," the stepmother recalled. "One thing that came up between him and me was the discussion of parties. I said, sure he could have parties. Then he asked if it was all right to drink beer in the house and I said, 'Sure, occasionally.' Then I realized that what he was really talking about was having drinking parties, and he admitted it. I said, 'Well, we'll have to grapple with that,' but the response I finally came up with was no, you can't do it. It was an unpopular decision, and it still is, but his younger sister, who visits twice a month, wholeheartedly supports this decision. My reasoning to him was, if it's illegal and you have kids over, I don't want to be put in the position of having to call every mother. I would prefer to avoid the situation entirely. I don't want you to get into a set of circumstances here at home which will get kids in trouble with their parents. Nor do I want to cause a lot of fear on the part of those parents that if their son comes to our house, he could come away drunk. I made the decision myself because I decided that was the way I felt comfortable. Although his father might have given a slightly different response, we place a great emphasis on the theory that if one of us says something, the other supports it, even if it might be wrong. We sort out our differences in private."

Doing what is comfortable for you and making the child know that this is the only way you can live with peace of mind seems to be the first and major key to family accord. It doesn't seem to matter if you are avant-garde or an old stodge, liberal or conservative, easygoing or meticulous, so long as you know what and who you are and help the child understand what makes you tick. If you can help the child understand why, that's even better.

Psychologist Frank Strange, in mulling over all the facets of getting young people ready to live with stepparents, says, "Theoretically, it's better for the adults to work out their relationship first before dealing with the children." Most of us, he feels, find it easier to work on a one-to-one basis, but if it's possible to hash things out within the dynamics of a family group, this has its advantages. "Some people can work on the whole-system relationship easier than others because of their own way of growing up—perhaps in a family relationship that acted as a unit. I think this kind of approach is very important because it's the basis of people getting along, and we have to recognize our interdependence with others."

He feels that the most important thing is to work on openness in communication, to put your expectations on the table and not to feel that you are holding back, that your expectations aren't so important, that you can work on them at some later date. "Rather than get hung up about what do I know about this young person or the young person's parent, you should make a conscious effort to let these other people know about you. You must take responsibility and say, "If you don't know some things about me that might cause trouble later on, it's not because you haven't been after me, it's because I haven't been open enough.' "

If one can feel that responsibility to be open strongly enough, and act upon it, that's the first positive step to adjusting your stepchildren to living with you.

What If Your Mate Has Been Widowed?

"I was looking for a loving stepmother, someone who would really understand me. So it was really nice to hear that I was going to have a new mother."—*a midwestern boy talking about his stepmother.*

"This isn't my daughter. She isn't today, she never was, and she never will be. I have stopped pretending. She remembers her mother and tries desperately to hold on to every memory."—*a West Coast stepmother talking about her stepdaughter.*

These are the extremes: the child who yearns for a new parent to replace the one who has died and the child who fantasizes about the dead parent to such an extent that there is little parental role allowed to the stepparent. If you are living with or preparing to live with someone else's child whose parent has died, the chances are that the reactions you get and the relationships you develop will fall someplace in between.

Don't assume that this is like the divorce situation, especially the bitter divorce situation, where you would be living with a child who bears scars of a tension-filled, traumatic household. The child of a widowed parent bears scars too, but they are of a different variety.

The aloneness of a widowed parent and child not only reinforces dependency but provides rich compost for culturing myths about the deceased. The longer a single-parent household continues, the more rigid the child tends to become about his memories of the dead par-

ent and that parent's claim on the living. It can lead to painful confrontation.

Mollie, whose stepdaughter, Karen, is now a teen-ager, recalled
that competition with her stepdaughter's mother started before the
child was five. "One day in the kitchen I reprimanded Karen for
something, and she looked at me and said, 'If I had my choice, what
mother do you think I'd rather have? My other mother or you?' "

A perfectly normal reaction might have been to lash back, giving
hurt for hurt. But she restrained herself. "I turned off the stove, and I
sat down and said to her, "Karen, you don't have that choice. Your
mother cannot come back to life, and I am here. Choice has nothing
to do with it."

Mollie was perceptive enough to see that she was being set up to
contest with Karen's dead mother and that she could never win. She
decided to remove herself from the fray. "I told Karen, 'It's time you
knew something. I don't want to take the place of your mother. I'm
just trying to take up where she left off. You know your mother is
deceased, and you only have her in a memory. So let's not talk about
which mother you'd rather have.' "

What Mollie was experiencing was the flowering of a normal reaction in a child whose parent has died. Some simply do not articulate
it in this manner. Psychiatrist Gordon Livingston says, "You can expect the development of myths and fantasies that seem to increase
with the years. As a stepparent you'll have to confront this as a real
possibility, and you should be prepared for the implicit and explicit
comparisons that the child will come up with between you and the
dead parent."

Mollie admitted that she hadn't always been perceptive with
Karen, that there had been a time when she thought Karen was trying to put her down instead of recognizing Karen's need to clarify
and identify her various relationships. "The one mistake I made was
when Karen was going through a stage of needing to tell people I
wasn't her real mother. I got upset, and I asked her, 'Why do you do
that? Why do you want to tell people I'm not your mother?' Then I
told her, 'I don't tell people you're my stepdaughter.' I realize now I
shouldn't have put it that way. I intimidated her by telling her she
shouldn't discuss this with other people, and I left her with no one to
discuss it with except me."

Not long afterward, though, Mollie realized that by trying to curb

Karen she had helped glamorize the whole subject. She took her aside. "I told her, 'Karen I want you to know that I think it's perfectly all right if you want to tell people I'm not your mother. You have a right to do that, and I want you to feel free.' " Then Mollie further defused the problem. She asked Karen if she wanted her to tell people that Karen wasn't her daughter, only her stepdaughter. "Well, the moment I asked her that, this need she had to tell people died down. It wasn't exciting anymore, now that everything was going to be out in the open."

In more ways than one, Mollie salvaged the relationship with Karen. It was apparent that Karen was building up the image of her dead mother to superhuman proportions. Idealizing her, Karen would often retreat to her room, where she would weep over old photographs. Mollie went out of her way to get Karen interested in the here and now, busy in projects, helping her to come to terms with reality. It is far from easy to be a stepparent to a child who feeds on fantasies and self-pity. Psychiatrist Willem Bosma comments, "Where a child continues to mourn a dead parent, the child's fantasy may have built the parent into something beyond the realm of comparison, and over the years, whenever a problem comes along, the child will blame the stepparent because the dead parent— who is close to perfection—could certainly never be at fault."

Another situation that a parent's mate will often confront is the child who has been the object of much sympathy because of the death of a parent. The frequent consequence is a child who has an exaggerated sense of his own importance, who retains the center of attention. It does the adult no good to sit back and let the child monopolize the stage—that's the way tyrants are tolerated. It's best to act quickly.

A Florida stepmother told us, "When I got Paula, she was queen bee. Her mother had been forty-two when Paula was born, and her father forty-five, and they had no prior children. From the beginning Paula was the light of her father's life, and he spoiled her, and so did many of their friends. The strange thing was that all these friends were childless, so when Paula arrived, it was a special event for them. Then, when she was almost five, Paula's mother died, and a couple of months later all the friends took Paula and her father to Jamaica for a three-week vacation, all expenses paid. Since Paula's birthday fell during that period, they even hired a calypso band for her party and lavished presents on her. For a little girl it was over-whelming."

Paula's stepmother wasted no time setting things straight when she became part of the household. "Of course I didn't just rush in and change things, but I knew she shouldn't continue in the adult night life she had been used to. Right away I could see she never liked to lose—whether at a game or anything else. I told her that wasn't real life, no one wins all the time. I guess I tried to impress my own standards on her, and I had very little trouble. Maybe she sensed that being fussed over was not the same as being cared for."

Sometimes the problem for the prospective stepparent comes in fulfilling the expectations of the child. The loss of a parent can punch such a hole in a child's life that the only way the child feels it can be filled is by replacement. Many children, however, especially younger ones, hope that the new parent will have the same characteristics, temperament, and attitudes of the dead parent. When this doesn't happen, disappointment can lead to resentment and trouble. Even if the child is very young, it's good to find out all you can about expectations and all the familiar habits carried from babyhood.

Stepparents, unlike parents, don't have the years of slowly gathered and ingested experience to help them fathom what goes on in the children's heads. They also seem to be afraid to talk and, most importantly, to listen to what their stepchildren have to say. Their expectations can be simple or complex. For some, they can mostly come true.

One teen-ager talked about his. "I guess what I really wanted more than anything else was a mother and brothers and sisters. My stepmother turned out to be the kind of person I always hoped a stepmother would be like. From the first moment I met her, she seemed to be a really good mother to her other kids, and they seemed like nice people. She's always friendly and talkative. This was going to be the family I always wanted, because I had been an only child, then living alone with my dad, and he worked nights. But after we all started living together, I had this doubt in my mind just exactly where I fit in, if they really accepted me as much as I accepted them. They have different ideas than I have, but I like that. I always wanted companionship, and I wonder if they like me. But it's kind of hard to just walk up to someone and say, 'What do you think of me?' "

He considered himself lucky, except for the doubts that he didn't mean as much to his stepfamily as they did to him.

Suppose There Is Bitterness from the Prior Marriage?

"It is commonly agreed by behavioral scientists that the separation and divorce experience is damaging to the child," states psychologist Hannah E. Kapit. "The wounds and scars depend on the child's constitutional make-up, his childhood experiences up to the actual circumstances of the conflict situation."* Yet, she concludes, damage is not caused by the separation and divorce itself but by the tensions leading up to the separation and the tension-filled events that come after.

The results on the child's behavior can be significant. You can expect some of the following to occur:

- hyperactivity
- nervousness
- ultrasensitivity
- aggressiveness

Conflict between parents arouses a child, and sometimes this arousal can get out of hand, creating chaos in your household. One stepmother whose eight-year-old stepdaughter is hyperactive relates what this can do to a family. Whenever the stepdaughter comes to visit, she affects not only the tranquility between her father and stepmother but also the family harmony for her younger twin half brothers. "She creates problems by inciting fights, taking toys away from the boys, and tripling the noise level. Even baby-sitters won't come when she's visiting."

Hyperactivity in this form—as a behavior problem—is highly de-

*"Help for Children of Separation and Divorce," in *Children of Separation and Divorce*, ed. Irving R. Stuart and Lawrence E. Abt (New York: Grossman Publishers, 1972), p. 202.

structive because so few people are prepared to deal with it. Some, such as this stepmother, see its devastating effects and resign themselves to a future without much hope. "The older the child gets, I think, the more difficult things are going to be. I'm really worried. There are years of misery ahead." Others, however, see only the disruption that the child's behavior causes. In trying to deal with it on the usual level of discipline, there will be disappointment and frustration.

Fighting is common among children whose parents are hostile toward one another. Anger breeds anger, and children turn theirs against brother and sister as well as against their parents. Sometimes the fighting is a sign of their own anger erupting at the sorry relationship between their parents, anger that they can only direct at other children. It might also be jealousy because the tensions have brought out one parent's favoritism, another's dislike. The children are on edge, and fighting is one form of safety valve. But it can be hard on a parent's new mate. "My two stepsons are close in age," says a Colorado woman. "They are highly competitive, and they tend to fight a lot. That really makes me uptight, because I can't take the constant picking and screaming, so the longer they stay with us, the worse it gets, and now, as it gets closer and closer to five o'clock on Fridays when they come to visit, I find myself tensing up."

Yet this stepmother can understand where the battling comes from—it's a reflection of the parents' attitudes toward each other. "What their mother does is grill the boys when they get home, and I know this because if there's something she didn't like, she calls up my husband and starts with the 'You can't do that to the children' or 'Please don't do such and such again.' Of course, the children sense the tension and act accordingly."

While most behavioral professionals will underscore that it is far better for a child to be insulated from a tension-filled, unhappy household—that separation and divorce in these cases actually serve the child's needs—there is one aspect that clearly rocks the child. Before the divorce, in spite of all the anger and hostility, the child was at least part of a family with a mother *and* a father living under the same roof. The emotional and psychological role models that the growing child needed were right there. There was no need to try to adjust to a new adult, no loyalty conflicts, no guilt feelings in the child that she herself might have been the cause of a split-up.

"In so many of the stepfamilies I have counseled," says psychologist Frankie Mae Paulson, "there are common themes that create problems between children and parents. One is this business about loyalty to the other parent. 'Is is okay to take in someone new? Does this mean I have to give up someone else?' Even in divorces where one parent was punitive and destructive to the child, I think we make a mistake when we assume the child will be better off with a new stepparent who might be kinder, more understanding. We forget that the child may have in his head a fantasy about the other parent, a myth about the way it was . . . so the fantasy parent can become more important to the child."

While a child's loyalty can be one obstacle to a good relationship with a new adult parent figure, another is often guilt, or the assumption of blame for the parents' breakup. A child will ask himself questions like, "How is it I don't have the parent I had before?" And that will translate into, "Is there something wrong with me, is there something I did?" Ms. Paulson continues: "It isn't only emotional, but it's cognitive as well. Children tend to be fearful that their own impulses, angers, even wishes may have caused that person, that parent to go away. So if the child feels he sent one parent away because of an impulse, he is going to be very fearful that his impulses are going to get out of hand again."

The child's reactions will take one of two directions. Either she'll hold back in any relationship with a new parent figure—even someone she might be strongly drawn to—saying to herself, "I don't want to get involved again," or she'll act out a role, moving close, testing the adult and saying to herself, "I'm going to see if it happens again." In both cases the child remains on the defensive, and it's going to be up to the adult to work the relationship into anything meaningful.

A particularly nasty consequence of a bitter divorce is the rigidity it places on custody and visitation, and it doesn't matter whether the child lives with you or just visits from time to time. The hostility between the parents produces a competitiveness that forces each to deny to the other anything that will provide an edge. There is basic distrust and suspicion about the other's motives whenever any changes or modifications are sought, and the only certain way not to be outdone is to keep things as they are. Yet while the parents maintain their standoff, the child is in the middle, and sometimes it's difficult for them to understand.

The child may cop out or drift along. "Four years ago I felt that if I really stood up and said I wanted to stay in my father's home, I could have," says sixteen-year-old Craig. "Personally, I wanted to. But I didn't want to cause waves. I didn't want to get the families uptight, though today, if I had it to do over again, I would have stayed with my father and stepmother."

What's it like in the middle, between two warring families? "I think my mother believes my stepmother is trying to force her out of the mother role, and this bothers her. And my stepmother is irritated because she feels she is being pushed out of the stepmother role, and it's a vicious circle. I really get caught in the middle, because I love them both. What I try to do is stay a son to each but not get overly involved with either."

Though Craig lives near several good colleges, he plans to go to one clear across the country, more than three thousand miles from home. "I feel it would be to everyone's advantage if I were far away for a while and did not have to shuffle weekends."

His weekends are especially burdensome. "I do feel bound to divide my time between my parents. I'm supposed to alternate exactly even. At one time I may owe one parent a few hours or half a day. My mother makes me very aware of this. For instance, we had a big argument because I wanted to go to my father's house early a few weekends ago, since I had the day off from school. My mother reminded me I already owed her half a day that I must pay back."

Quite often when a child comes for visitation or comes home after an extended stay with the other parent, it takes awhile to shift gears, to become attuned to the new household. Craig's mother and father live about an hour apart, and that helps. "The bus ride between houses is necessary. When one or the other parent picks me up, I don't fit in for two or three hours."

Other stepchildren have told us they feel like Ping-Pong balls going back and forth between their warring parents. One calls the train ride between homes the transition train, and another said he had to "unthink" about the house he had just left and "rethink" about the house he was going to.

One thing appears fairly certain. The child will probably be uncommunicative for a while after arriving, and it's best to let him settle into the household at his own pace. It may not be apparent to an adult, but a child of dissident parents may be struggling to rid himself of the tensions of one home and to steel himself for the other. "I change my whole self when I go from one to the other parent," said Craig. "The basic belief structure that upholds my mother is different from the belief and moral structure that upholds my father. I have a basic me at the bottom, so I try and shift my face plate, so to speak."

Unfortunately, there are situations where children may be so scarred by the bitterness between parents that they just become unlikable. Even their parents find it hard to love them, and for the mate of such a parent the question can become one of survival. No one should be deluded into thinking there are happy solutions.

- *from a stepmother:* "I suggested that my husband seek custody of Harriet, but I'm sure I was motivated by revenge against her mother. Harriet would probably be in a better situation if she lived here. But me? I guess I would retreat to the kitchen, where I go now every time she visits. It's become the cleanest room in the house."
- *from a stepfather:* "We have an understanding. I don't speak to him, and he doesn't speak to me. If we want to communicate, we go through my wife."
- *from a stepmother whose stepchildren have only visited twice in six years:* "They simply don't concern me. It's as if they are some distant, unlikable relatives of my husband's. When and if they come to the house, I make it a point to stay away, and I never think of talking to them on the telephone."

The bitterness from the prior marriage can hurt a parent's new mate as well as the children. A Washington stepmother described how what was to be a happy wedding day for all the new family turned sour at the end. "One horrible part about being a stepmother is that a vindictive ex-wife is *always* part of your husband's life. You just never get rid of her until the kids are grown. Well, when she remarried, the kids went to her wedding, but then she decided they couldn't come to ours. So my husband met with her husband and talked to him. He said, 'Don't worry, they'll be there,' and they were, but she put up a terrible fuss. The night before our wedding we had a big family dinner, and my husband was really depressed."

The wedding itself went fine, the reception cheerful. "But we had to drop the kids off at their mother's before we could start on our honeymoon. She insisted that no one but my husband could do that. It infuriated me. The oldest boy said to his father, 'If mommy starts yelling at you when you get in the house, just walk out,' and I thought, 'That bitch, she plays up being such a marvelous mother and this is what she's doing to her own children.' Sure enough, he walked in, and she started screaming."

It requires super strength and empathy for a nonbiologically related but concerned adult to come to terms with such bitterness and the wreckage it causes. But you're well advised not to join in and add a dimension to the war. It's in the interests of both the children and yourself to be above the fray. Psychiatrist Gordon Livingston says, "The more conflict there has been and continues to be from the separation of the parents, the worse position the kids are put in. Some behave in very destructive ways because of this. The best advice I can give stepparents is for them to stay out of these conflicts as much as possible."

What Do You Do with an Inherited, Live-in Housekeeper?

"I've never seen a live-in housekeeper who was inherited from premarriage days work out in the long run," says psychiatrist Willem Bosma.

This statement was seconded by other professionals and stepparents, yet some of the stepparents seem to have done their best to make a bad situation worse.

The callous and immediate firing of a housekeeper is sure to have unfortunate repercussions. Bosma concurs. "Recognize that she has been almost a psychological parent in many cases. The children should not have her snatched away completely but be encouraged to visit her. I recommend, though, that she not continue in the household." Bosma believes that children can quite easily accept the fact that when a new parent comes into the home, the housekeeper will go, if it is presented to them early and rationally.

By early, Bosma means before the marriage. A most unhappy incident happened to one family with the sudden and unexpected expulsion of the housekeeper. The three children in the household were presented with a new mother and the loss of their housekeeper on the same day. They had been quite attached to the housekeeper, and over the prior four years she had become the psychological parent referred to by Bosma. But the stepmother, in her ignorance of the children's deep attachment, could not conceive that they would miss her. She now considered the children *her* wards and the house *her* territory. She took no time to find out the household routine or what special techniques the housekeeper employed to handle the children.

The children were immediately resentful, she recalled. They were undoubtedly bitter, or at least she interpreted their remarks to her in that manner. "For weeks afterward," she said, "the kids would say to me, 'This isn't the way Miss Helen did it' or 'Miss Helen tells us to do it this way.' I snapped back at them, 'I don't care what Miss Helen did or didn't do or did or didn't tell you. This is the way *I* do it.' Looking back, I suppose letting the housekeeper go that first night we got back from our honeymoon was a mistake. The kids seemed to resent me from that moment. But I was going to be a super mother and do everything myself. I gave up my job to spend full time at home. Again, looking back seven years and the dreadful relationship I had with those kids, I probably should have kept working full or part time and kept the housekeeper for a while, then eased her out and got someone of my own. Or else eased myself gradually into the job of mother and housewife. I just didn't know any better, and it has really made our marriage lousy."

Psychiatrist Hans Huessy reckons that anyone who is going to be a stepparent in a situation where death or illness has required the children to be taken care of by a housekeeper had better move quite judiciously. "Certainly you have to be careful when replacing a previous housekeeper. I think you must work your way in and become acquainted, certainly not bounce in and take over. A housekeeper can be most important to the household."

This applies not only to the child but to the father as well, we learned. He may have come to count on her heavily, and that relationship shouldn't be disregarded. A quick and heartless dismissal shows an insensitivity that could undermine family relations for years.

A successful transition was described by a stepmother whose inherited housekeeper had worked in the household even before the five-year-old stepdaughter was born. The housekeeper was an older woman and had taken on the aura of "grandma." The stepmother had already raised her own daughter and had been widowed. She was a secure person, successful in her business and not looking to the stepchild to gratify her emotional needs. There was no deep desire to be queen of the roost, no overwhelming need to make this daughter "her own," undoubtedly because she had already raised a child. She recalled the three years the housekeeper lived with her and her new family. "She was a lovely woman, and my husband never could have managed without her in the years after his wife died. He's really quite helpless around the house. I needed her because my business kept me out of the house much of the day, and I had neither the time nor the inclination to become an instant maid. I also needed her to watch over my stepdaughter and keep the household running smoothly. My stepdaughter was used to taking orders from her, and I was glad to turn over some of that responsibility at first. The housekeeper did the grocery shopping, and I did the cooking. We all ate together in the dining room, so you can see she was quite close to us. But as time went on, I could see that she was not able to relinquish any control over my stepdaughter, and I found more and more things I wanted to help her with or correct her about. Another problem was that no place in the house seemed big enough. The laundry wasn't big enough, the kitchen wasn't big enough."

As this stepmother became more secure, she became less willing to share her domain. It was time to make a change. "It boiled down to the fact that I felt it was an invasion of family privacy. By this time I had adjusted to having this family and wanted to take more of a hand in everything."

So this stepmother spoke to her husband about dismissing the housekeeper. "I realized he had never thought in those terms, but I told him that our life would be more well rounded when we became a closer family. It was a blow to her when she had to leave, but we arranged that she could do all the baby-sitting, even to sleeping over from time to time, so the break was gradual."

While this stepmother had felt freer to go her own way when the housekeeper was in the home, she was willing to forgo that to take on more of the family responsibility and control. "Once she left, my relationship with my stepdaughter improved too. She no longer had to listen to two people and sort out authority figures."

Although each housekeeper situation has its unique aspects, sharing a home with someone who has been looking after the children before you arrived in the house can bring tensions, perplexities, and often outright trouble. In many instances the housekeeper has become the child's psychological parent, and this bond is not easily broken or replaced. Most professionals seem to agree that an inherited, live-in housekeeper should go, but the method, as well as the timing, of dismissal should be humane and objectively motivated. If you were in the child's place, would you want it any other way?

2
FULFILLING
EXPECTATIONS

Behavior and Discipline

Discipline and authority are ever-present sources of crisis in all stepfamilies. "They are *the* issues upon which children and parents pivot their difficulties," says child psychologist Jean Chastain. It's safe to say that where a stepfamily hasn't worked these matters out, the family is in dire danger of coming apart. "Who is in charge here?" is another way of putting it, and where the parents are undecided, you can be sure the child will take advantage. Remember, the behavioral professionals tell us that children—every child—is an opportunist, so when the parents haven't established a positive pattern, when they have set no limits, who can blame the child for moving to the path of least resistance?

Most families must deal with a common set of circumstances, though the responses may vary widely. The following were the most frequently cited and should be regularly revived:

- *money*, who distributes it, when, and how much?
- *manners*, who sets the style?
- *chores*, what, when, and who?
- *curfew*, who sets it and when might it be changed?
- *family car and telephone*, who uses them and when?
- *smoking and drinking*, who, what, when, and where?
- *television*, when and how much?
- *punishment*, who dishes it out and in what manner?

The first step is to recognize that behavior expectations for the children must be set, or you are bound to have chaos. It's not only a matter of maintaining some semblance of order within your family; it's essential that the children grow up familiar with what society expects of them. Otherwise, they will simply fail to function as adults.

Dr. Brandy Adams, family doctor and therapist, advises that the more explicit you are about what you expect and the more you bring things out in the open, the better off you are. "It's best done by both the stepparent and the parent talking it out among themselves, getting their act together' first, so they can have a consistent set of expectations." Then you sit down with the children and work out the details. Adams feels that the stepparent should be in the picture from the very beginning and that both parents should discuss the matter with the child, "so the kid gets the endorsement of the natural parent and gets the feeling that the stepparent is right on the team."

Adams breaks the various behavior expectations down into "positive" and "negative" types, believing that the major four or five of each grouping should be worked out with the children. "Positive expectations," he says, "are those you wish the children would do. It's behavior you want from them, and you may have to motivate them in this direction." Examples include, "I wish you would wash the family car twice a month" or "I expect you to baby-sit for your little sister one night a week." Negative expectations, as you might imagine, are those items of behavior that you wish the children won't do, such as, "I don't want you to eat with your fingers" or "I don't want you smoking pot in the house again." Once you've established your primary positive and negative expectations, you can feel pretty confident that the children will know what the ground rules are.

Sometimes, though, it isn't so easy to effect behavior expectations. You and your mate must recognize that each has to support the other, or the child might end up receiving two distinctly different messages. This is particularly true for a stepmother, who, according to sociologist Gerda Schulman "is even more dependent on and in need of her husband's support. The reason for this need is that the stepmother is a newcomer to an already formed relationship and is seen both as a rescuer as well as an intruder.* Where the husband is

---

*"Myths That Intrude on the Adaptation of the Stepfamily," *Social Casework* 53 (1972): 134.

weak or passive person, allowing the stepmother to take the lead with the children, the chances are that the child will deeply resent it, and the stepmother will feel overwhelmed and quite angry. In these circumstances there may be behavior expectations, but it will be extremely difficult to make them work.

This happened between Connie and her stepsons. She had never been married before, and she and her husband, who had been widowed for several years, dated for almost a year before they decided to marry. The boys were ten and seven at the time, and before the marriage Connie had been more like a friend to them than anything else. "Sometimes we even dated as a family," she recalled. But Connie was dissatisfied with the boys' discipline, although she never mentioned it until after the wedding. "The boys expected I would continue to be friendly and buddy-buddy," she said, "and they were really surprised when I became a disciplinarian overnight." Her husband was surprised too, and it caused a great rift in their marriage. "My husband doesn't like a heavy hand, the boys resent me, and I don't know how to ask either my husband or the boys for help." Everyone is losing here, but it could have been different if they had realized that discipline and authority are matters best worked out ahead of time. Even Connie sees it now. "If I had it do to over again, I'd sit down and explore those areas before we got married."

From the child's view, the failure to work out behavior expectations can bring confusion, hurt, and a sense of hopelessness. Trusting to the dynamics of marriage and living together for the expectations to work themselves out is not always successful. A teenage stepson told us, "The major problem was that I had been on my own for a long time, an only child living with my father. I was used to coming and going as I pleased, and then all of a sudden I get a new stepmother, and I have someone telling me I had to be home at a certain time, that I must do this or that. I would get into some awful arguments, and the thing was, it all seemed to change overnight."

No one had explained to this boy ahead of time how things would be different. Everyone just assumed that matters would take care of themselves once the family became a unit. But additional problems developed because the stepmother never squared away her expectations of her stepson. She had three children of her own, reared quite differently from her stepson. He said, "She always tried to compare me with them, saying 'Why can't you study like them?' or 'Why can't you get dressed like them?' " It disturbed him very much, to the point where he gave up trying to do anything. "I told her, 'I'm myself, and you can't change me into something I'm not.' " But for two years, this boy who was unable to order his life, became a constant drug user. It took professional counseling to help him come to terms with the family situation and neutralize his need to retreat.

Among the questions you will have to ask yourself are: Will you tolerate verbal abuse? Is your mate going to jump into the argument? Do you expect a response after speaking once, twice, three times? How much argument will you allow? How close a relationship do you expect from your mate's child and he from you?

A stepmother from Ohio who is now a family counselor went into her stepfamily with no time to work out expectations. Twenty-four hours before the children arrived their mother announced she was turning them over. This was just a week after the new marriage. She recalled, "When we first got the children, their father was over-protective, especially of the eight-year-old girl. We had some arguments over that." The stepmother didn't want the father jumping into the battles she was having with the children. "If I had a fight with my stepson, I wanted it to be *my* fight. I wanted him to let the boy and me have our own relationship. The same with my stepdaughter." What she was asking for was enough latitude to show each child the limits of the opposition she would take and the scope of what she expected. "I told my husband, 'I can't be close to the children if you don't let us grapple. When I'm angry at them and tell them to go to their room and they say no, I want you to let me handle it.' My husband finally realized that he had to let the children and me work through our problems."

It's true that when you set out to establish your behavior expectations, you will probably meet with opposition from the children. The opposition, as with the Ohio stepmother, is also a form of behavior that must be worked out. Occasionally, you will uncover reasons that can't be discounted or even dealt with.

Kathryn, a young Massachusetts stepmother, has two stepsons, aged seven and five. They live with their mother but visit Kathryn and her husband every other weekend. From the moment Kathryn first met the boys, she was appalled at their lack of manners and their disrespect for other people's property. "I've tried to sit down with the kids and talk about how I expect them to behave in my house or in anyone else's house," she says. "They sit there and agree, but then they really don't follow through." At first Kathryn couldn't believe they wouldn't respond, and her frustration grew and grew. After all, she couldn't be any clearer about what she wanted. Even her husband supported her. But finally she realized that their mother's influence and their young age made it onerous for them to meet her expectations. "I think it's because they just don't have a long attention span, and I suppose they really are too young to understand much of what I want—especially when they go back to their mother and aren't subjected to the same demands as I make on them." This isn't going to stop her, however; only her sights will be lowered and her patience extended.

Once you've worked through behavior expectations, you can expect them to be tested and retested by your mate's children. It's a part of the child's need to explore the limits of the relationship you are developing. Psychologist Bernard Steinzor writes about the child of divorce and his need to test the stepparent. It must happen "before he accepts the reality of the remarriage, which means essentially, the reality of the divorce."* Your response will determine how long the testing goes on. "When the stepparent makes his presence felt and shows the child that he is in the home to stay, the child will, with great relief, simultaneously accept him and give up his wish to unite his divorced parents."**

You must recognize the testing for that it is and respond with restraint and understanding, as the stepparents did in the following two instances:

- *from a stepson:* "It took a hell of a lot of effort to call my stepfather 'dad.' But it really happened after a fight one night. I was in ninth grade and watching television late when he and my mother came home, and he made some comment about my being in bed, and I snapped back and bristled. He said that maybe he ought to slap me down, and I doubled up my fist and told him to try it. He was about 270 pounds and I was about 140 pounds. He immediately calmed things down and walked off,

*When Parents Divorce, (New York: Pantheon, 1969), p. 199.
**Ibid.

and I felt foolish about it all, and it wasn't long after that I
started calling him 'dad.' "

• *from a stepmother:* "In the first months there was a lot of testing
by both boys, usually by being obnoxious to each other or
refusing to cooperate with me when I asked them to do
something. 'Do I have to?' or 'I don't want to' were the usual
responses. So my husband and I talked about it and decided that
whenever it happened again, I would send them to their rooms
for a specified period of time. After they went to their rooms
about a half dozen times, the whole thing just settled out."

Once the testing period is over, you should have established a set
of behavior expectations that will see you through the long pull. By
this time the expectations themselves will have been tested for their
usefulness, and all of you—stepparent, natural parent, stepchildren,
natural children—should have a good idea of what will be tolerated
within the family. In this you will have fulfilled the hopes you
started out with. To reach fulfillment, however, you will have to
arrange your own conduct to generate the behavior you are seeking,
and in the final analysis you really can't expect much from a child
unless you are willing to point the way.

From the many comments by stepparents, we think the following
show some appropriate ways to fulfill your behavioral expectations:

• "We aren't the sort of people that feel that just because a child
does something in the morning, we have to wait until dad gets
home at night before there's any punishment. So if there is any
discipline needed, I take care of it at the time it needs doing."

• "I've never been criticized for disciplining my stepchildren, and
I've never been questioned on the things I've done. So it never
has been as if I'm taking on someone else's child, but rather as if
they are part of me too."

• "Try to be fair in terms of disciplining the children and set up an
expected pattern and stick to it. Achieve a certain consistency,
such as, if this is bad one day, it's bad every day."

• "One day my stepson commented to one of my adult friends,
'That's the most ridiculous thing I've ever heard,' and I immediately reacted and said, 'No way can you speak to friends of
mine like that.' I felt the remark was gross enough to demand an
instant retort from me."

- "I expect my stepsons to be responsible, and when they aren't, it affects me personally. One of the first things I did was to make a job list which they could check off when they had done their required chores. It meant there wasn't any question about when the work had to be done or who had to do it."
- "I understand the role I play in my stepdaughter's life, and I give her different things than her mother does. I lay out values for her and talk about the future and what I want from her now and in the years ahead. We speak about morality and responsibility, while her mother provides her with material things."

Will Your Mate's Child Love You?

Our expectations are like wagons hitched to the stars. They can take us to the grandest heights providing they don't distort or obliterate reality.

Fortunately, our growing sophistication about realities in interpersonal relationships has made us a little less dreamy-eyed about children—and stepchildren. We know from child psychologists that children have specific needs at different stages of development, that their behavior goes through stages, that their orientation is basically self-serving. Although this is a meager guideline, it helps us to look with more objectivity at our stepchildren and to understand why they feel as they do.

You can expect the children to resent you, says Jean Baer in her book *The Second Wife*. Not love? ever? Of course it's possible. Stepparents and stepchildren we talked to admitted as much. But resentment at one time or another in varying degrees seems to be more prevalent than love. We can only assume that, given the right circumstances, with the proper amount of empathy on all sides, love is possible. Not always probable, but possible.

The age of the child when you first start stepparenting has much to do with it. And this has nothing to do with gender. A baby or very young child responds to nurturing stimuli and will form an attachment to the person who cares for her. If you are loving, the baby will develop loving traits. This premise seems to be the consensus of professionals who have studied and written about the subject over the last generation.

Stepparents themselves feel the same nurturing response to the tiny child. One stepmother who cared for a four-month-old baby over the period of a summer (this baby had been born after the parents were divorced) finally told the father that turning the baby back to his unstable mother for intermittent periods would not work. She herself couldn't bear the emotional drain of relinquishing the baby whenever the mother was lucid enough to care for him. The child is now seven, lives with the stepmother, and visits his mother. As far as the stepmother is concerned, their relationship is as strong as a blood tie. The child identifies with the stepmother, loving her as any child would a natural parent who attended to his needs from babyhood on.

Most stepparents are not lucky enough to be given responsibility for a baby, who can grow to become a part of them. Instead they get young children, whose personalities and traits are somewhat stabilized, or older children, who are most certainly reluctant to express love openly, even if they feel it.

A young child and a stepparent have a common need. They are both vulnerable and need emotional nurture. The stepparent craves approval and acceptance, and so does the child. Yet stepparents find it hard as rock candy to limit the disciplinary role. In fact they seem to challenge, "If you care about me and my feelings, you will do the things I require." The child, on the other hand, is looking for real praise and approval. She knows she's been pretty good in her father's and mother's eyes, but what is she in the eyes of her step-parent? If she's an unlovely child, it becomes even harder for her. And never doubt for a moment that a child knows when she's unlovely. She may be scrawny, buck-toothed, uncoordinated, a stutterer, and therefore, doesn't love herself very much. If she hears you bragging about one of her accomplishments or gets an honest boost of praise, it will lessen her feelings of self-worthlessness and leave her more open to respond to the person who does approve of her.

Instant love, however, is not the goal or even the reality here. Sociologist Gerda Schulman refers to instant love as one of the two recurring myths in stepfamily stories (the other being the myth of the wicked stepmother) "the reconstituted family, fantasies and hopes play larger parts than in the ordinary family. . . . The child has already incurred a loss that not only creates greater vulnerability but tends to increase and stimulate the fantasy of the perfect mother (or father). The adult stepparent, who is a figure in the fantasy, tends to react irrationally to the messages inherent in the child's behavior partly because he too is vulnerable."*

Reacting irrationally to the messages that emanate from our mate's children is as common as birdsong in May. But it may not sound like birdsong to the child, who withdraws to ponder the effect of what he has said or done. If he didn't mean to act as badly as it came off and the adult doesn't understand that, the child will conclude that the adult doesn't want to understand. Vulnerability assures one thing: It makes all of us nervous about leading with our chins. This applies to the unsure child as well as to the unsure adult.

Sometimes a child's conflicting identity will keep him at arm's length or even mildly hostile toward his stepparent. This identity, says psychiatrist Willem Bosma, is a complicating factor for a child of divorce. "He would feel guilty in giving up his real father, for instance, and loving his stepfather more. Frequently, not until the child is an adult and these pressures are off him can he say, 'Tom was an awfully nice guy to us and did more than my father did.' Before adulthood he probably would not admit this because of guilt that he's betraying his own father."

A girl who has now followed her stepfather in a medical career had many reservations about him when she first started living with him. She found every reason in the world to be mildly critical and not let herself become fond of him. Her own father, she said, "was very cool, self-possessed, unemotional, and careful about his emotions. I was used to my father, and I thought it was a measure of dignity to maintain coolness. My father was an impeccable dresser. My stepfather was none of these things. I was used to my father and didn't think my stepfather was as much a man as my father was." It was years before she could allow herself to express the warmth she felt for her rumpled, concerned, and interesting stepfather. She believes, now, that her original standards were false, yet it was

_____
*"Myths That Intrude," pp. 131, 132.

probably her maturity that brought her to love and admire her stepfather without guilt. In the young person's world of absolutes it is almost an impossibility to separate love from loyalty. And while a child may feel very guilty about not loving a parent, no such taboo exists toward a parent's mate.

While it is well known that babies and very young children "love" in response to fulfillment of their physical and emotional needs, this also carries over into youth and even into adulthood. How long would you stay in love with your mate if he neglected your physical and emotional needs? If a stepparent becomes the main source of security for a child, then kind feelings will naturally flow in that direction. Another adult stepchild, looking back on the years of security that his stepfather provided, said: "In making my life with my stepfather, I really worked at it." He was nine when his mother remarried and ended the years of drunken fighting and one-night stands. "I wanted to work at it. It was a way out of a bad situation, and he created a stable household and did the things a father normally does. I'm glad I didn't go into it thinking I'm going to try and get that guy out of here, as some kids try to do. It worked to my advantage to be respectful and good to him. When he died, I was really broken up."

Children, in the most pragmatic sense, have a survival instinct. They'll hang in with those who can help them and ignore, or even undermine, those who threaten them. These needs extend into adolescence and in some cases beyond. Lewis has an incompetent, alcoholic mother whom he has not seen in two years. His father died more than a year ago, and now, while he finishes his education, he continues to live with his stepmother. He would be most reluctant to give this arrangement up. She represents the only family he has, and he says he feels closer to her than to his own mother and admits that he loves her very much. If his own father were still alive, if his mother were a different type of person, he might not feel this strong bond with his stepmother. But it's these "ifs" that often make the difference.

The stepchild who is simply a visitor in your home may never feel love in any ideal sense. Although some visiting stepchildren are more standoffish than others, their feelings are generally quite ambivalent. One says, "Outside of the fact that my stepmother has helped me get along better with my father, we're not that close. I like her. She's a good person. But we don't try to make it more than it is."

Making it more than it is, hoping that the child will love you because you are the stepparent, can be the source of torment, or at the very least, plain disappointment. Children are quick to sense when unnatural pressures are being applied. As another step-daughter remarked, "My dad just can't understand why we can't love my stepmother as much as he does. We play the game, but that's all it is."

Perhaps the word *love* should be stricken from a stepfamily's lexicon. Since the family situation is artificial, even at best, we might do better to lay aside the emotion-fraught words *love* and *devotion* and substitute *like* and *respect*.

When expressions of affection do spring from a stepchild, they are apt to be infrequent and a long time coming. Randy, who is a full-time stepfather to his wife's teen-age daughter, was surprised, pleased, but still not overwhelmed when his stepdaughter finally got around to expressing affectionate appreciation for his attention and concern. It happened one night during a party he had helped her set up for her friends. At this point they had known each other for years but had lived together for only the past two years. In that time, though, Randy had taken over as much of a positive father role as he could. "I went down to the rec room to check the ice and see if the kids had enough sandwiches and drinks, and my stepdaughter came over to me in the hall and told me how much she loved me. It was the first time she had ever done that. She said, 'You really are a nice guy. I get mad at you sometimes, though.' I said, 'Well, I get mad at you sometimes, but I guess you know by this time that when I say the things I do, it's for your own good.' She said, 'I know that.' Then she gave me a hug, and that was the only demonstration of affection between us."

Most professionals are uncomfortable with a stepparent's need to be loved by the children. Psychologist Frank Strange commented that he doesn't think we should entertain this expectation at all. "I believe the love thing is a crazy question anyway. I'd rather say you should earn their respect and hope it leads to something else. If you feel good about yourself, knowing you're doing the best you can, trying to be respected as a good person, then if love comes along after all, it's a bonus."

Another psychologist, Dana Lehman-Olson, sees the expectations of love as a constricting and even dangerous element in stepfamilies. "When people have to deal with the multiple tasks of marriage plus the issue of intimacy, I think, the focus of trying to legislate intimacy is the area that creates the most problems." Drawing on her experience, she adds, "The single most common mistake I've seen people make is to put pressure on one another to be related in certain types of ways rather than to let those relationships emerge as they will. I don't think you can create or make people feel a certain level of closeness to each other." Experience shows that forcing or expecting people to act as if there is a love relationship when there isn't can even cause the breakup of the stepfamily.

One young man who has had, aside from his natural father, two stepfathers and assorted half brothers, half sisters, and stepbrothers and stepsisters recalled what emotions he felt toward each of them. The word *love* did not surface. He saw, instead, his stepfamilies as "an accident of circumstance that brings a group of people together. Out of this some relationships have developed pretty well, and others have gone to nothing."

How Much of a Parent Should You Be?

"However strong the stepparent's determination to be a parent—however skillful his efforts, he cannot succeed totally," write two psychologists.*

The stepparent role is like a piece of clothing. We may long to be comfortable in it, but all too frequently we end up with something that looked good for the moment or something that evoked a pleasant image or something urged on us by a manipulative salesperson. We become so hung up by how we'd like to look or should look that we neglect to remember who we really are.

In stepparenting, knowing who you are is fundamental. Finding

---

*Irene Fast and Albert Cain, "The Stepparent Role, Potential for Disturbances in Family Functioning." *American Journal of Orthopsychiatry* Vol. 36 (1966): 488.

this out doesn't happen overnight, nor does it take on its full bloom until you are involved with the family.

Psychologist Frankie Mae Paulson believes it is the first step in deciding how much parenting you are capable of, how much you want to get involved in the lives of other people's children. She says, "I think people assume there is something they ought to be doing, and they don't really get in touch with how they themselves feel as a parent. Any woman who becomes a stepmother, for instance, should know whether she's a maternal kind of person, know her capacity to give, to share, to tolerate feelings of other people. Unless you are able to do that, you are not going to get a reading on the child or be able to understand where the child is coming from. You'll constantly be responding to superficial kinds of behavior."

Knowing who you are may not enlighten you about all the nuances you can expect, but it will give you a touchstone from which to operate. If you've never been a parent before, then becoming part of a stepfamily is like being a substitute teacher. Hassles will erupt from all sides. You are vulnerable because you are an outsider. The regular teacher, like the natural parent, knows his class, the limit of his tolerance, the level of his endurance, and the idiosyncrasies of the children. This is not to say that his class or family life may not be disorganized. It well may be. He may be looking for the "substitute" to bail him out for a spell. Probably you will not want such a situation on a steady basis, but a lot of step-parents unknowingly move into that role.

Unwittingly, Virginia, at the time of her sudden ascension to stepparenting three teen-agers, was manipulated into the substitute role. (Now as she goes through analysis, she realizes that she wholeheartedly embraced becoming the mover and shaker within the household.) She said, "In my husband's first marriage he was the reliable strong person who kept things under control as chaos swirled about him. When we got married and the kids moved in, the role of the person in the middle switched to me. He liked being the hero and avoided taking a stand. Whenever there was discipline to be done, I would have to do it. He'd say, 'You tell the boy,' or 'You do such and such to the girl.' I found myself asking him how well I was doing with the kids and was I doing the best for them. He constantly praised me, telling me what a wonderful job I was doing. My poor stepdaughter got the brunt of it all. I was constantly after her to work and act up to her potential. She was such an intelligent and talented person that I wasn't going to allow her to limp along. Since her father never stepped in, I'd be on her back, telling her she had to be the best she could be. Sometimes I'd break down in tears at the response I'd get, and I'd talk to my husband about it, and he would tell me that I gave so much of myself. He said, 'Let her know why you're giving so much.' In fact my stepdaughter hated me outrageously for three years. I finally backed up and stopped passing judgments all over the place, so the two of us started to work out a better relationship together. Now that I think back on it, on all the times I'd ask him how well I was doing with the kids and he told me what a wonderful job I was doing, I was doing him a disservice and a disservice to the kids. I never insisted that he jump in the scene. Instead I let him stay outside and play Mr. Wonderful."

Virginia, whose capacity for love and involvement is tremendous, was ready and willing to take over her husband's "class." He was ready for a sabbatical. But Virginia's role was destined to self-destruct because she did not know what the parameters of possible involvement were. Every stepparent faces the parameters of possible involvement sooner or later, and these determine how much of a parent you should be.

If there are two sets of stepchildren in a home and both sets of natural parents are living and taking part in their children's lives, then for the stepparent to adopt a "mom" or "dad" role is ill advised. As a parent, you must meet the needs of *your* children. As a stepparent, you should only supplement what the children get from your counterpart.

A pair of stepparents discussed how they perceived the extent of their parenting of each other's children. Jill said, "It's obvious that my own children have different needs than my stepchildren, and I try to fulfill each on an individual basis. For instance, my thirteen-year-old stepdaughter has been reaching out for someone nearer her own age to take in interest in her personal problems. She has a thorough understanding that I don't wish to take her mother's place, yet I'm a good friend and she's become a good friend of mine. From the beginning I've made it clear to my stepchildren that even though they live in the same house with me, I would not take on a "mother" role. Being someone who cares is what counts."

Since Jill's ex-husband is still involved with the children, although more on a personal than on a financial basis, her husband, Michael, said, "I don't want to become the father to my stepchildren either. I see myself in the role of friend and provider, a person who shows interest in them, one who can provide physical and psychological needs, but basically I like to see them have a good relationship with their real father, one that will continue."

Dr. Benjamin Spock said twenty years ago, "My hunch is that almost every stepchild, even though he develops an excellent relationship with the stepparent, will want to continue to think of this as different from his relationships with his own father or mother."* This was confirmed by our talks with stepchildren. Whenever the relationship was pushed into artificial parenting, the children backed off, and their emotions ran the gamut of guilt to anger.

Unlike Michael, there are many stepparents who, because they have had their stepchildren from infancy or because the other parent has left the scene, are inclined to assume a stronger parenting role. And this is the way they like it. They want to be part of the governing board of the household. As one stepfather looking back over ten years of stepparenting said, "I think if their real father were around, it would have undermined my authority and stature in the family. I feel it would have been a real handicap to the second marriage."

But sometimes the other parent is just barely in the wings—ill, incompetent, unable to raise the child or relate to the child as a normal parent would. At times like this there would be the temptation to become the complete parent. This happens most often with stepmothers who take over small children. How do the successful ones handle it?

"I've had to be very careful not to deny their real mother to them," said a young Idaho stepmother. "I thought everything was going along smoothly for a couple of years. She was glad to have me take over the responsibility until the day the older boy called me 'mommy' in front of her. She freaked out. There were absolute hysterics, and I realized that she could only comprehend my mothering them on a certain level. On that gut level she was the mother. The boy never made that mistake again, nor did I let him get in the habit of calling me 'mommy.' The little one, oddly enough,

Problems of Parents (Boston: Houghton Mifflin, 1962), p. 247.

can call me 'mommy' without infuriating her, probably because he was born during the divorce, and she half denies his existence."

This stepmother does not have an easy time drawing the line between wanting to be a total parent and an "almost" parent. But the more she involves the natural mother, the less confusion the children feel. They are not being forced to deny, hate, or ignore their real mother, and this leaves them free to love and rely on their stepmother. Their own mother has become something of an indulgent aunt, lavishing expensive presents on them, taking them on exciting outings. "I feel I should do what I can to ease the relationship between them and their mother," she said. "I don't want them to grow up and have hang-ups about her. If I get really angry, I wait until the kids are in bed, then I ventilate to my husband, who understands how frustrated I can get."

Psychologist Margaret Doren agrees that it's necessary to hold back from the temptation to take over as parent. "I think one of the dreadful things about stepparenting is the confusion it can give the child about where he belongs, and that's why I think it's important for the stepparent not to take over the position of parent. If a child has to deny one to accept another, he's faced with an intolerable choice."

But sometimes a child *will* try to deny his natural parent and look at the stepparent to take over completely. Earl, whose mother had excessively abused him, has refused to see her for the past three years. He wants his stepmother to be his real mother. How does she handle it? She said that even though she feels as close to him as if he were her own, even if she'd like to erase the face of his mother off the earth, she knows it would be self-deluding. Earl knows how secure he is with her. Yet his mother still exists. She is a fact. And Earl's stepmother will not take advantage of the boy's fear and dislike of his mother to capture him for her own, to become the total parent. "I try to talk to him, to get him to remember the good things. While I can't force him to like her any more, I urge him to be a little understanding about the hard times they had and that these might have contributed to his bad memories." One thing is certain, Earl couldn't love his stepmother more if she were his natural mother, and her delicate way of keeping him in touch with his real past will help him avoid questions and guilt when he grows up.

The new mate who comes into a household where the child has

been alone with one parent for a long time is faced with different barriers to becoming a parent figure. On the one hand, your mate may say that he or she wants you to take a hand in all decisions and discipline, but when it gets down to the nitty-gritty, or if things aren't going so well between the two of you, this understanding may go out the window. You find yourself being countermanded and ignored. It is imperative that you recognize two things: The child has been managing with one parent, and it will take many slow steps for you to be considered a parent figure. Even if, with all the generosity in your heart, you want to make the child yours, provide for her and become her benefactor and confidant, you are whistling "Dixie." Whatever parenting you do will be by the grace of your mate, the child, or your own good cautious sense.

The second thing you should recognize is the motive behind your mate's wish that you become the parent figure. The motive is usually distaste or bitterness or all-out hatred of the former spouse. He or she has been chucked out of the picture, but don't be deluded into thinking you can supplant that parent quite so fast.

The wise stepparent doesn't just give up all authority and retire or cop out. But he or she learns when to confront and when not to and how much parenting the stepchild will tolerate. There's no reason that you can't make policy decisions with your mate, but it may be easier to let him or her handle the verbal instructions. One stepfather remarked, "I get the kind of behavior I want, but I don't come out and demand it directly. I go through her mother. For instance, if it's a school night, I'll remind my wife that her daughter should be home early, then she tells her when to come in. Even after two years I'm careful about giving my opinion, advice, or counsel the way a father would. I figure she lived without me for twelve years, and I'm not sure yet how much guidance she's ready to take from me."

Of course most children are not ready to be parented right off the bat. This is not to say that they won't be amenable to following the rules of the house, but they resent forced intimacy or the assumption of many adults that parenting comes before mutual trust and friendship. Psychologist Jean Chastain cautions new stepparents not to be overeager. "Don't try too hard, I say. Don't worry about it so much, don't be tense or uptight. Usually if you can relax a little bit and just enjoy the child and get to know him, it will work out. How else are you going to achieve a positive relationship with a new person except to take the time to get to know him and enjoy him for what he is, not for what he ought to be?"

How much stepparenting you should do is a constantly shifting thing, and the degree or intensity depends upon those parameters of possible involvement. The adult who doesn't come on too strong stands a better chance of becoming a positive force in a child's life, if that is what you would like to be. Yet even adults who have raised children whose natural parents are dead have said there is a certain block beyond which your words are not heard, your remonstrances not heeded. Is that the end of the line? You've raised a stepchild over the years, and slowly, slowly you are trying to lead him to interests and habits that are compatible with yours. He balks. He is still not your child. And you cannot, no matter how hard you want it to be, ever become his parent. Almost but not quite. If you're a woman, it's harder for you, say the professionals, because so many of you want to be super-moms. Many women erroneously believe they need to prove themselves, by being as much of a parent as they know how. It's sad. It's also bad.

Stepchildren offered us a host of memories about their step-parents, the kind things they did, how they helped them in a shaky or hostile world, friendships they formed. The need for a total parent never entered the picture.

- *a teen-age boy talking about the last four years:* "I felt a little down when my father told me he was going to get married. I thought I was an important part of his life. We hunted, fished, went to ball games together, and I was afraid all this would stop. But as it turned out, we do more things now, because my stepmother likes sports more than my own mother. She's like a mother part of the time and has been helping me get ready for college. But I'm not as close to her as I am to my own mother. Still she helps me in lots of ways my mother doesn't know how."

- *another boy talking about his second stepfather:* "Sometimes he would pick me up from school and often wait half an hour. He would go out of his way to do things for me that he felt I needed, even if I didn't ask him."

- *teen-agers talking about the man who lives with their mother:* "He doesn't mind taking us anyplace we need to go. He fools around with us like another kid and helps us with homework—all the things our real father never took the time to do."

- *a high school senior:* "I always thought of my stepmother as a little bit of a mother but mostly a friend. She gives me help because she's not emotionally involved with me the way my mother and father are."

"How much parenting?" repeats a psychiatrist. "I would say, move very carefully." Dr. Hans Huessey, himself a stepfather, looks for something beyond parenting. "I feel it's very important for children to develop long-term adult relationships outside the home. We're so tied up with the concept of the nuclear family. Yet part of raising children is to help them develop meaningful adult relationships besides those with their parents. These people can tell them all the things a parent can't and show them things they need to know."

Many stepparents are comfortable being just a friend, and many stepchildren wish there were more stepparents who were.

Should Visiting Stepchildren Conform to Household Rules?

One stepmother says, "If my younger stepson is going to come into my home from time to time and be a part of it, he's going to go by our rules. It's not fair to his older brother, who lives here all the time, that we change things to suit him."

Another stepmother says, "I figured the younger girl would only be with us for a short time, so why bother with too much discipline and training? Rather just let things ride, because she would be gone before long."

These are two stepmothers with stepchildren approximately the same age, both with an older child living with them and a younger child who visits from time to time—and attitudes diametrically opposed. There's good reason for either approach. If you *do* make the visiting child conform, household order will be retained; if you *don't* make the child conform, you won't have to face a struggle each time that child comes to visit. But what about the effect on other members of your family? what will it do to the overall atmosphere inside your home?

When we're talking about household rules, we really mean those limitations we place on a child's behavior. Depending on the child's age, rules can cover—

- responsibility for chores
- sharing toys
- respect for possessions and property
- time for meals and appropriate table manners
- personal grooming
- watching television, when and how long
- destructive behavior
- use of the telephone
- keeping one's room clean

Generally, the professionals with whom we spoke felt that a stepparent—or a parent for that matter—is safer in expecting the visiting child to conform to household rules. It eliminates the potential problem of resentment from the other children, and everyone in the family knows what to expect from every other person. In this sense, at least, family harmony will be preserved.

In her book *The Second Wife*, Jean Baer offers a number of suggestions to a stepmother with visiting stepchildren. Though much of what she has to say could apply equally to the stepmother with a full-time stepchild—or to the stepfather, for that matter—she does advise—

- "know that you are mistress of your house and act accordingly"
- "you have every right to express your own values."*

What she is really proposing is that the adult is quite within his or her rights to *expect* the visiting stepchild to conform to the rules of

---

*(New York: Doubleday and Company, 1972), pp. 56-57.

the house. It isn't a question of *if* but *when,* and the adult has the option of deciding that.

A California stepmother described how she went against the wishes of her stepson's natural mother when problems arose while the boys were visiting. "When the boys lived with their mother, she felt my husband—their father—should not interfere in any way with their discipline. Then, when they visited us, she said over and over that we should treat them like guests, their father shouldn't discipline them even in his own house." This stepmother recognized that the boys' mother was motivated not by any major interest in her sons but by a desire to eliminate their father as an influence in their lives. "So we just went ahead and disciplined them anyway."

For some visiting stepchildren, conforming to household rules is what they really want, because being treated like a guest doesn't help to make one feel a part of the family. The child stays an outsider, somewhat in limbo with respect to relationships with everyone else in the household. It's the uncertainty of it that bothers children, and an uncertain child can easily become an insecure one, not trusting even the friendship offered by the stepparent. Another young stepmother recognized these feelings in her stepdaughter and worked to give the child the family interaction she was looking for. "Joyce has no sense of loving care in her home environment," she said, adding that Joyce lives alone with her natural mother while her brother lives with her and his father. "In her mother's home, she performs many chores, makes her own meals, and generally takes care of the house." At first this stepmother thought Joyce might prefer to take it easy when she visited, since so much was expected of her by her mother. But she quickly found just the opposite—Joyce didn't want to be a visitor, she wanted to be a full member of the family. "So when she visits, she helps clean up the kitchen, she dusts while her brother vacuums. Then, when we all sit around the table at dinner, she just loves it. It's the whole family relationship that she misses with her mother."

Where there is already another stepchild living with you, the relationship between that child and the one who visits is certain to be influenced by whether you insist the visiting stepchild conform to the household rules. Anytime one child can get away with something at the expense of another, there is bound to be ill feeling. "For a while I wasn't sure what to do," says an Ohio stepmother, "but then

I realized it just wasn't right for either of my stepchildren to be treated differently." So she went ahead and told the younger child he would have to abide by the rules of the house, even though he came infrequently. It has worked out well. "The major adjustment has been for the older child, who has to change from an only child to older brother whenever the younger one comes." The older boy helps the younger know what's expected of him. Each has certain responsibilities, and there appears to be no ill feeling.

There are some, however, who suggest that it isn't necessary for a visiting child to toe the line, that in some ways it is asking too much from a child who knows he's a visitor. Of course, if the child lives close enough and visitation is open enough so she spends a good part of her time in your house, then she should be considered practically another member of the household and treated accordingly. But what about someone who only comes occasionally, possibly from a long distance? Says psychiatrist Frank Strange, "One question I generally ask any stepparent who may be discussing the visit of a stepchild is, 'What if it wasn't your stepchild but a foreign exchange student, a person with a very different background than yours? Would you expect him to come in and behave exactly as one of your natural live-in children?" To Dr. Strange, the real issue is whether you can get to the point of convincing yourself that behaving differently makes sense. If it does, then you can bend your rules, knowing that you aren't acting arbitrarily. Each of the following instances might be appropriate for this:

- where there is such a wide age difference between the children that few legitimate comparisons can be made
- where the visiting stepchild has such deeply ingrained habits that you couldn't possibly break them during the visitation period
- where the visitation is for short and infrequent times

Perhaps the most effective way of dealing with the child who is visiting is to base your actions on the length of the child's visit. The shorter the visit, the more you should tend to treat the child like a guest, asking and giving respect and courtesy but not expecting an inordinate amount of work. This is what psychiatrist Hans Huessy recommends. "When the children visit on weekends or holidays, it should be a special occasion, and they shouldn't be required to compete with children who live with you on a day-to-day basis." He believes, however, that where the children will be around for more than a week, it wouldn't be fair not to expect the same from them as from the children who live with you.

Rules are the framing for civilized society. In your own home you've made them for mutual protection and comfort, and they should serve your visiting stepchild as well as the rest of you. Yet only you can ascertain whether the true purpose of your household rules is to make things more livable for everyone or if in fact they could become snares left lying about to trip up the unwitting and unwelcome visiting stepchild.

Suppose You Never Raised a Child Before?

We found a number of common experiences among stepparents who had never been around children of their own.

- They harbored myths of instant love, and when nothing materialized in their own hearts or from the children, they became disappointed and resentful.
- They often found themselves in rivalry with the child.
- They were apt to be rigid and stern disciplinarians.
- Childish behavior mystified and annoyed them, and they frequently described the children as hyperactive.
- They assumed a parenting role too quickly, yet were resentful of the other parent's implicit obligation to the child.

The expectation of instant love is most common among younger women. When they suddenly take on a young child, especially one whose other parent has died, flights of fancy seem to sweep away all rationality. One of the most poignant disappointments came to a woman who had had three stillborn babies from her first marriage.

Her widowed boyfriend had an adorable daughter, something of an angel during the brief time they were courting. The stepmother said, "When I met Mark, it was like the answer to a prayer. Here was a ready-made family. I entered into it more than fifty percent ready to raise and love this beautiful little girl. I'm sure if Lori hadn't gotten along with me while her father and I were just dating, Mark wouldn't have married me. But Lori preferred me over other girls he had dated. I think now that I may have married him for this four-year-old more than for himself. I know now that I tried to make her everything I didn't have—a child of my own. I would raise her just as I would my own if they had lived, dress her up, curl her hair, turn her into a well-mannered, lovely young lady."

Where did the beautiful dream turn into a nightmare? This stepmother was prepared not just to offer but to inflict love and attention. She became the instant mommy, trying to bend the child to her ways. "I love you," she told Lori, "you're my little girl." It didn't take long for rebellion to replace Lori's last vestige of good behavior. "I'm daddy's little girl," she finally squeezed out, "and I don't love you."

Lori's refusal to reciprocate devotion soon turned to active challenging of authority. Within two years both the girl and her stepmother disliked each other. Lori's stepmother finally had to face up to the fact that Lori was not her child, never could or would be, and if they were going to live in some kind of harmony, she would have to come to terms with their relationship. She backed off, deciding Lori needed only her occasional rather than constant involvement. With the holding back, things improved. Now, nine years later the two are friendly and usually enjoy each other. Yet Lori's stepmother feels that her life as a surrogate mother has been unsatisfactory. Her expectations were so great. "I had such potential love to give, if only I had a child of my own to receive it." She can't let the myth die, nor does she grasp that the need to love and be loved is not the same as loving. The first can be a trap, the latter an occasional miracle.

A stepfather who discovered that the miracle of loving never existed said, "If I had it to do over again, I would let the relationship with the kids gradually develop over two or three years before I'd take them on. I would never jump into a marriage with stepchildren. The more time you have to see how attitudes change and develop, the better. I think many of us who have never had our own kids should realize that those kids with the smiling faces probably don't like you at some level. They resent some other father or mother coming into the situation. The reality of not expecting reciprocal love is something you have to recognize and deal with."

Rivalry is as bothersome to stepchildren as it is to the stepparent. Kids can't understand why it should be so. They think, and rightly so, that the new stepparent ought to realize that there *was* another marriage, that it *did* produce children, and that these children have a right to their parents' time and attention. "Please understand," said a new young stepmother to her husband's teen-age daughters, "we just got back from our honeymoon. I want to be alone with your father for the next few weeks and don't appreciate your coming over to our apartment." The older girl retorted, "We haven't seen him for weeks. You don't understand. You married a man with children, not a bachelor."

Rivalry with stepchildren seemed most prevalent in stepfathers who craved most of their wife's attention. Sociologist Gerda Schulman says, "In the great majority of families in which a previously unmarried man becomes a stepfather, the man was very dependent on his family (usually his mother) and therefore . . . liked the thought of a woman with children and thus, in a way, married a 'mother.' In his relationship with his stepchild he is both identified with the child and in rivalry with him."* She deduces that the "dependent" stepfather is usually more interested in his wife's capacity to mother him than in being a strong father. With girls, these men often have flirtatious relationships.

Unfortunately, we can't turn rivalry and jealousy off like a faucet. The reasons go deep into the past. But if we come to terms with the realization that we do rival our stepchild's bid for time and affection from the parent, then we've made a start in understanding the mutual resentments that are bound to develop.

Joan, a stepmother with no children of her own, had a very young stepdaughter who visited weekly. Almost from the beginning Joan resented sharing valuable weekend time with a small child who meant nothing to her. She had no maternal memories of her own to make it easier for her to understand her husband's feelings for his

---

*"Myths That Intrude," p. 132.

child. Yet she didn't dislike children. In fact she liked them and always wanted a couple of her own. But this child was a different cup of tea. Her behavior struck Joan as distressing. Since Joan was unsophisticated in the ways of child rearing, she didn't realize that there are usually obvious reasons for a child to act as he does. And although Joan knew that her husband's first wife loathed her and blamed her for the divorce, she didn't know that three-year-olds can be thoroughly brainwashed. Three-year-old Annie displayed every symptom, yet Joan didn't catch on. "When she first came to visit, she wouldn't let me touch her. I thought this was strange. I had never done anything to the child, and it was the first time any child had reacted to me in this way. Most of the time she stayed cuddled up in her father's lap. I was jealous. I knew it was pointless, asinine, and dumb, but I couldn't help it. I was also jealous that she'd go to him and not me." As Annie got older, a few of her mother's hateful comments slipped out, and Joan began to figure out why Annie had felt it necessary to spend almost all day in the protective arms of her father, and why she wouldn't let him out of her sight. She was purely and simply terrified of Joan, whom her mother had portrayed as a wicked stepmother. If Joan had already had a child, she would have been in a better position to know what was going on. But all she knew was that she suddenly seemed to be a rival of a three-year-old, and she didn't like the feeling one bit.

Those who have never raised a child before tend to be rigid and stern disciplinarians. Women are just as likely as men to be strict, though men seem to lean more toward physical discipline. Gerda Schulman describes the type of man who, marrying into an already existing family, suddenly behaves in an autocratic manner. She postulates that in his early years he was an "antifamily" man, prematurely independent, acting the adventurer but later settling down, wanting to make up for lost time and unconsciously hoping for respectability. By the time he settles down, he has repressed his own antisocial or infantile impulses and now rejects any childlike or acting-out behavior on the part of the stepchild. The mother, Schulman found, and we also found this to be the case, is often intimidated by, but in need of, the man and sacrifices the interest of the child to keep peace in the family.*

*Ibid.

But what of the parent's mate who simply expects and demands no-nonsense behavior? Psychiatrist Gordon Livingston also finds this most prevalent in people who have never had children before. Either men or women, especially younger ones who take on a family of two or three children, can easily find themselves unreasonably harsh in exacting behavior. This, unfortunately, is the role that too many stepparents fit.

Psychologist Dwight Mowry deplores the fact that these new-made parent figures take on their tough and exacting role with such vigor. Ideally, he believes, a person who has not had his own children when he starts to share a life with another person's children should set out to be a positive influence. "In other words, do many pleasurable and instructive things for and with them. Then, when you do give them commands that they fail to carry out, there is not only the punishment aspect of the outcome but also the withdrawal of nice attention from someone who is becoming important in their lives. You must adapt to their world, watch them while they perform, play games they can win. Then you will be on firmer ground when it comes time to handle bad behavior at the table or at bedtime." Mowry cautions that you may still feel like an outsider, but the responsibility is on your shoulders to adapt. At the same time, if you want to change their behavior, you're going to have to do it over a period of time. Most important, you must first become a positive influence and friendly entity to them.

Understanding childish behavior is inordinately difficult when you haven't gone through it with your own children. It's like dealing with little creatures from another planet. We heard so frequently that the children didn't act or respond the way the adult expected them to, that they snooped into drawers; fingered things; fidgeted in restaurants; bounced in their chairs; were withdrawn, sulky, monosyllabic, gluttonous, picky, fractious, demanding, loud, mumbling, whining—and most frequently "hyperactive."

The "hyperactive" complaint occurred so many times that we asked a child psychologist what she made of it, and she said that it's a catchall word used frequently by those people who don't know kids well enough to differentiate between the pathological child who can't sit still even to eat and the youngster who won't sit with her hands folded quietly for half an hour. A bewildered adult may not know what's within the range of normal behavior and may think he's got a real squirrel on his hands. So it is most necessary to supplement one's knowledge of child behavior by comparing notes with other parents and stepparents, by getting professional help, and by opening up communication with the natural parent.

Unfortunately, you can't know through osmosis that the child might have the traits of a certain grandparent or could be a fixer like her uncle, the engineer, or a dreamer like his aunt, the artist. For want of any cogent understanding, those of us who have never raised our own kids put labels on others. But it's cheap and self-defeating and begs to be corrected.

Jumping into the stepfamily whirlpool and almost going under is the fate of many "uninitiated" parents. You're going to be the best you know how, take on the PTA, mend that dress, teach them to fix a flat tire, hand out advice right and left, try to win the child over. If you had already been a parent, you would know this gets you nowhere. Children go where they want, feel what they want, move in the direction that makes them most comfortable. If you were the natural parent, you would have developed the relationship slowly, through the years, from diaper changing to trips to the doctor to visits to the circus. You can't become an instant parent and make up for lost time. When you offer to do these things, you should realize that the children might not want it thrust on them. They'd rather get their parent—the one who has already been through it with them—to do it. It's natural.

One very young stepmother, who had never had any children, recalled her terror when she learned that an eleven-year-old son was going to move in with them. First, she was shocked, then scared, then wondered what her role should be. Should she quit her job? be a super mom and take over the natural mother's place? She almost did, but some still voice kept whispering, "You'll be sorry," so she slid gently and calmly into it all and let the boy's father take over most of the parenting that the boy needed.

And what's her role? "I guess you could say I'm like a favorite aunt, respected, liked—even loved—but in no way could I be confused with his mother."

3
THE OTHER FAMILY

Seeking Out the Other Parent After Many Years

The denial of painful experience is a common phenomenon. We quickly forget the hurt of an accident, for instance, and naturally tend to insulate ourselves from unpleasant remembrances, relationships, and events. Dredging them up are what psychiatrists' couches are for, because we certainly try to put them behind us. This putting-behind process goes for the absent spouse as well, the no-good s.o.b. who, through a biological accident (or so we wish), fathered or mothered a child you are now trying to raise.

But there is a stirring interest in children to find out more about a parent they may not have heard from or seen in years. If the interest isn't already there, the chances are that it will be someday. Many stepparents seem to feel threatened and more than slightly insulted and they wonder as honestly as possible if it's really such a good idea. There are adequate, even overwhelming reasons for a child to look up a long-gone parent, and there are also many reasons for reluctance, both on the part of the child and on the part of the custodial parent.

Psychiatrist Gordon Livingston looks at the positive side from the young person's point of view and does not regard it as a threat. "I see it as perfectly natural for a child to seek out an estranged or lost parent for a number of reasons, especially for getting information about heritage. Yet, with the increasing publicity that the search for the biological parent is getting these days, a loyalty conflict develops, both within the kids and between them and the parents. I think this has to do with the view of children as one's possession, the 'after all I've done for you' syndrome. Yet the tie to the person who has provided day-to-day parental care is not going to evaporate on the basis of trying to find out about one's biological past. Step-parents should be more relaxed and supportive about this. If people don't use kids to fulfill themselves in such a way as 'we raised you, and you owe us this,' then there would be no big debt piled up."

We talked to many young people who had either sought out their parents or planned to. The reasons they gave were varied, although simple curiosity was the most frequent. A past half lost in fantasy and a hope to bring substance to elusive myths also spurred the seekers. Sometimes the results laid the myths to rest. For a few it opened up a relationship that had been denied through years of enmity between the parents.

Carol is one whose stepfather assisted in reaching her father. She and her brother are four years apart, were born in South Africa, and lost contact with their father when Charlie was three and Carol seven. Their new stepfather brought them to the United States with their mother and younger sister. "Carol was about eleven or twelve," their stepfather recalled, "when she started talking to me about her father and what he was doing and what the possibility would be to get in touch with him. I guess her mother would have none of it, so Carol came to me. She wanted to know if I could help her locate him. I got the address for her and mailed the first letter off for her. I didn't feel particularly troubled by this, because he was so far away, and I didn't think there was any real chance of him becoming involved with the kids."

Carol recalled, "I wrote some letters to him, and he wrote back to me. I wanted to see him, even though I had been adopted by my stepfather at that time. But it was far away and cost a great deal of money. I got the impression that my father didn't want to have me visit, so I stopped writing to him." She said she still wants to go back to South Africa someday, because that's where most of her relatives are, and she might see her father, but it wouldn't be the primary reason for her going. Her brother, Charlie, has no remembrance of their father but says he'd like to meet him because he wants to find out what kind of a person he is.

Dr. Livingston, who supports such contact, says, "Advocating the idea that one should, or even can, sever contact with the non-custodial parent is a denial of a basic human need. It is unrealistic."

Dr. Margaret Doren is in accord. "Children want to find their identity, and I think they should be encouraged to do so if they bring it up." Finding a new relationship as well as one's own identity, however, is often put off until children are out of their teens. Why do so many wait this long? Dr. Doren feels that an underlying reason for the reluctance to make contact sooner is a timidity in facing this stranger. "There's a great deal of fear connected with the decision to discover your own identity. Yet as young people get closer to marrying age themselves, the importance of knowing as much about their heritage, especially before they have children of their own, overcomes the fear." It also follows that what seems impossible to a teen-ager becomes less of a problem at twenty.

The search for a grown-up relationship with the absent natural parent seems to be more prevalent among those whose custodial parents demanded or encouraged the lack of communication or whose custodial parents despised and attacked the other parent. Loyalty becomes a second factor in putting off the search until adulthood. The professionals' view is that a child has a great loyalty toward the custodial home and will go to lengths not to disturb that status quo or security. Even if one doesn't openly say, "I don't want you to see your father (or your mother)," this attitude seems to come through to the child. Psychologist Jean Chastain talks about families where the noncustodial parent has been pushed into outer space. She finds the at-home parent often telling her that the other parent isn't interested, doesn't make contact, doesn't want to have anything to do with the child. "In fact," she says, "if you probe a bit, you'll find that many times the absent parent has been purposely cut out of the picture. This is the area when an iceberg is very operative, because the parents show only their most concerned side, while hiding all those negative feelings and those reasons they would like to have proving the absent parent is no good. Instead, they put it on the basis that the absent parent doesn't send cards, doesn't send support—or too little support—and just isn't interested. To the extent that a psychologist or psychiatrist can make the parents aware of what they are doing, they can be helped. But there is no way a child can be kept ignorant of the natural parent without sustaining psychological damage."

When a child and an absent parent do finally connect, the outcome can be quite favorable, as the following instances attest:

- *from a stepdaughter:* "It was really interesting meeting my father because I didn't remember him at all. He was such a nice guy, and I'm glad to know he isn't such a louse."
- *from a stepson:* "After fifteen years of living in turmoil with my mother, I began to think that if I don't like her, maybe my father wasn't such a rotten person after all. I called him on the phone and asked him to have lunch. Since that time, I've seen him every couple of weeks for the past five years. I remember looking at him across the courtroom when my mother asked for more money. He never glanced at me, but my stepmother used to look daggers. Now that's over with, and they've become close relatives and friends."
- *from a stepdaughter:* "It was my father who took the initiative to see me. Over the years I felt we were better off without him because his letters made my mother cry, and when he tried to visit us, my grandfather ran him off the farm with a pitchfork. He writes to me, and I write back. I'm interested in knowing more about my background. My father's people are Mormons, and they're big on genealogy, and I want to pursue this. I want to know where I come from, including the Indian blood in my heritage that I think they want to hide."

Psychiatrist Hans Huessy sums up a fair generality. "If the absent parent is decent—not necessarily someone you or your mate like—then I think children should be assisted in getting to know him or her. Not only is identity important, but reality is always better than fantasy."

But there can be exceptions. Some children can be so traumatized by the brutal behavior of the noncustodial natural parent, inflicted either on them or on their other parent, that not only do they have no interest in renewing the acquaintance but they actually try to avoid it.

"My mother is really terrified that my father could track her down through me and threaten her life," says one young man who went so far as to seek out distant relatives and get his father's address. "He was a longshoreman, and her stories and my memories are not that good. Her fear is real, so as long as she lives I wouldn't pursue it. Perhaps after she dies . . ."

Another young girl was encouraged by her father to keep in touch with her mother, who was heavily into drugs and alcohol. The daughter was faithful about writing, although the mother couldn't pull herself together enough to answer. The father ruefully remembers that he even encouraged his daughter to go across country and visit her. When she arrived, the girl found a completely debilitated and incoherent person who stumbled through her days and nights. Their roles became immediately reversed, with the teenager taking care of her mother, tracking her down in bars, cleaning up her messes. The girl informed her father and stepmother she could not come back, that her mother needed her, and she must stay. "If she had been an emotionally strong girl, or even a few years older, she might have handled it and come out all right," her father related. "But this had the smell of a suicide pact. The mother had been bent on self-destruction for years, which of course an unsophisticated teen-ager couldn't assimilate." So the father and stepmother followed the girl and convinced her to come home.

Behavioral professionals seem to agree that, barring fear of physical or psychological damage, a child should be encouraged to make contact with an absent parent. Dr. Brandy Adams related his own experience and the conclusions he has drawn from his psychiatric practice: "I consider it a universal urge for a child to want to seek out his natural parent. In my own case my father died when I was two, and while growing up, I heard fantastic things about him. I went back to the little town in Wisconsin where he was brought up and took the time to go through the newspaper files and find out what I could about him. In my practice I find that the patients who have the greatest difficulty getting out of psychiatric therapy are children who were raised in well-adjusted, loving homes but have a sense of rootlessness from not knowing one of their parents. We all have a tremendous urge and curiosity to know where we come from, yet we really don't know very much beyond a few generations, even though anthropologists say we go back at least three million years."

The children tell us it's their immediate forebears that matter the most.

Should You Tell the Child Disturbing Facts?

A tightrope walker crossing Niagara Falls has an easier time than a stepparent who tells the kids hard facts about the other parent. There is only a slight distinction between opinion and information, between self-serving motivation and the honest desire to help the child or clear the air between you.

Child psychologist Jean Chastain cautions, "When you attack a child's loyalties, you are attacking the child's basic structure. Depending upon the degree that you are successful in making a child more loyal to you than to his other natural parent—whatever the faults—you have undermined the child's ability to cope. If this kind of criticism goes back and forth between both sets of parents, you get a child who is so distressed and torn up that he can't even cope with the problem of trusting anyone. Trust becomes dangerous to him because he feels that if he trusts anyone or loves anyone, he may have to end up being disloyal. That is a very painful thing to handle, and it brings lots and lots of guilt."

She is talking about the indiscriminate and venal use of "disturbing facts" as a means of turning a child away from her parent. It is fair to say, too, that what is a disturbing fact to one person may not be so to another. Philosophical and social differences do not constitute disturbing facts. Moralists, in particular, have narrow views about what constitutes acceptable behavior, and their criticisms are usually subjective and mischievous.

But beyond this, how much, if anything, should you talk about with your stepchild to help him deal with a sick, psychotic, or destructively bitter parent? Many professionals say, "You should work it out with the child." Others say, "It's a no-win situation for the stepparent. You may help the child but probably won't enhance her feelings toward you." A few say, "Stay out of it. Let disturbing facts be told by your spouse. The stepchild has a natural bias against believing you, figuring you've got an ax to grind."

Our talks with stepparents who have dealt with such problems indicate that if you're honest, understanding, and stick to the truth, there's a good chance you can be helpful. Alcohol, drug addiction, and extreme emotional difficulty were the areas where stepparents felt they could be most helpful.

Some stepmothers almost become big sisters or surrogate mothers when it is their counterpart who has these problems. The children gradually see their stepmother as an understanding, supportive friend who can separate the illness from the person. The kids come to realize that their natural mother isn't bad or ugly or no good, only sick. One stepmother retraced the steps she had taken to work through this disturbing problem with the kids. "When I first got to know my stepchildren's mother, I was very jealous of her because she was so pretty, but then I realized she was an incompetent alcoholic. The children had been with us for a few months, and I kept my remarks about her confined to the bedroom. She would call me on the phone and ask for help, sometimes from a bar or jail or at the garage because her car had broken down or she had had an accident. I ran errands for her and took her grocery shopping. I couldn't help but feel sorry for her. I gradually started to explain a little bit about alcoholism to the children and what kind of behavior they might expect. Whenever the children visited her, she would cry as the time neared for us to pick them up. They'd come home shaking, pale, and weak. So their father and I would sit down with them and explain over again. It seemed to take a long time and many talks before they could grasp the picture of alcoholism. I'm sure they didn't want to think of her as being hopelessly sick. They wanted a solution, and it was hard to face the fact that there was none. Now when they visit, they just let her go on and on, and they don't get worked up about it."

She summarized the way she tried to work through the problem with them. "I tried to be open and honest, and I tried never to assume that their mother hadn't been a good person or that she hadn't made a positive contribution to them and the way they were brought up, the way they think and do things." She discovered that the children's mother had some fine qualities, and by letting the kids know about these, they could better deal with negative facts.

Psychiatrist Gordon Livingston is one of the many professionals who believe that children can well understand that people have problems, that parents can act irrationally and still care. He says, "The important part of the message to the child is that it's the parent's problem and not the child's problem. Often when a person behaves in an irrational way, the tendency, especially for the child, is to assume that the cause falls on him. The inclination and, of course, the destructive part of a child's relationship with a parent like this is to think, 'There must be something wrong with me.' " If you can clarify that the other parent's yelling, crying, broken promises, forgetfulness, and even abuse stem from a problem within himself or herself, then you have been a big help to the child.

"It is much better," agrees psychologist Margaret Doren, "to recognize that their parent is sick or under great strain rather than be told or think the parent is a bad person. As the children grow up, they can forgive her if she is ill. Unfortunately, explaining disturbing facts about the other parent is usually not done in that gentle and sensitive a manner. The parent is pictured as hateful and vicious, and it's very destructive to the child to think that he came from a bad seed."

The children we talked to were always on guard against angry or subtle criticism of their natural parent. One girl who learned to like her stepmother quite well suddenly had a reversal of feeling because of this. It was over financial matters, she recalls. Rightly or wrongly her father and stepmother long harbored the idea that they were being "had" financially. The stepmother had never said anything about money before this, "until I came to their house one day, and we talked about my brother's college tuition. She jumped in and said there was no reason my father should have to pay it all, that my mother didn't have any money sense and was greedy. I became furious with the way she put it and decided to leave because I was too upset. I resented the fact that she criticized my mother without knowing how hard she had to work or without knowing all the facts."

Launching an attack like this drove the possibility of any rational discussion right out the window. The stepdaughter's defense was the most natural reaction in the world. Someone important to her was being attacked, and it was, in effect, an attack on a part of her.

Another stepmother handled financial "misrepresentation" with much more grace, yet her motives were not to help the children truly understand their other parent but to set the record straight about their father. "I finally felt it was important to get facts on the table. Their mother was telling them that their father deserted *them*, that he didn't care for them, that they were in a tough financial position. We knew that was totally untrue. They still had their home, enormous support payments, alimony, all medical bills and transportation paid. So I thought it was time I spoke up. There was no way I was going to let those kids hear that stuff without going to their father's defense. So I sat them down and went over the amount of money we were putting out for them each month. They were astonished when they heard this. First of all, the allegation that their father didn't care for them was given the lie. The second reaction was, what's mom doing with all this money? I have never made any value judgments about her because I felt that anytime I would say anything to the kids about their mother, I'd be cutting off my nose to spite my face. In this instance, however, I felt it was necessary. As the children got older, they began to see her bitterness and emotional childishness for what it was, and they would talk to me a little about it. It helped them understand why she misrepresented the truth. But at that time in their lives I couldn't let her continue without speaking up."

Children insulate themselves against parents' irrational or unexpected behavior, and it's generally agreed that stepparents ought to stay out of the picture if this is the case. It's up to your mate, if it's up to anyone, to deal with a child who is ignored, disavowed, or treated shabbily by his other parent. One teen-ager who visited his father after a ten years' absence found that he was an outsider in his father's new family. When his mother and stepfather picked him up after the visit, they noticed that the father had cleared the decks of his other children. The boy had met them for a few minutes to say hello, when he was introduced only as "Jim." On the drive home the stepfather wisely kept his counsel when the boy said he intended to visit them again. After three days of talking about spending holidays and a summer in his father's house, his mother said to him, "Look, I'm sorry to be brutal with you, but if he had been as welcoming as you think, then why didn't he explain who you were to those people who are your half brothers and sisters? I really don't think you have the kind of place there that you think you have. I don't want to hurt you, but I want you to face reality. Your dad told me ten years ago that he wanted to make a complete break with all of us and start a new family. This is what he has done, and I think you'd better back off to see if he feels comfortable accepting you."

The boy's mother said he didn't bring up the visit again, hasn't heard from the father, and she thinks that he took her explanation in the spirit she gave it, which was to protect him from a deeper hurt of not understanding why his father acted as he did.

One stepmother who has raised her husband's two little boys from babyhood has had a gradual chance to help them cope with their emotionally ill mother. She has been very careful not to tell them anything unfavorable about their mother and over the years has assured them that their mother loves them. Their stepmother has helped them through many broken promises and frenetic visits. She tries to protect them from hurt as much as she can. When they were very young, for instance, she never relayed promises of gifts or visits, knowing that rarely would they be realized. "I tried to keep the promises from them, but if they came directly from her, there wasn't much I could do. I wouldn't tell them she was coming to visit until right before the time she was to arrive. Once she was due at six thirty, and when I hadn't heard from her by five thirty, I figured she'd make it, so I told them she'd be arriving shortly. At six she called and said she couldn't come because it had started to snow and she couldn't make it. The older boy, who was already picking up on her disability, said, 'How did she know she couldn't make it?' The younger one now says, 'I sure wish she'd send those shoes she promised,' and the only way I can help them is to explain that she has a hard time fulfilling promises."

These children are still quite young. What about when they get older? "If they ask direct questions, I'll answer them truthfully. I think I learned from my work with other young people that if the parent's behavior or problems affect the kids, then the problems should be shared and discussed with them. The children should know what they can expect in erratic or aberrent behavior. But it must be treated as something separate and in as noncritical a way as possible."

The consensus? Tell the children about disturbing facts if your integrity or the situation demands it. The results can be a gamble, but if your telling is not an extension of your hostility, then it's worth the risk.

What If the Child Harbors Myths?

Our daily lives are fraught with myths. It is remarkably hard to stick to the truth, because humans not only tend to perceive things differently but also reject those things they don't wish to hear or know. Stepchildren are especially vulnerable to myth building, and some will go to great lengths to preserve and protect them.

When an adult takes over the care of a child one of whose natural parents has died, he often has to contend with the fantasy that the child has built around the dead parent. Not only are there few things more invincible than a myth, but it is the toughest kind of competition to deal with. How much you can expose fantasy, how you can go about doing it, and whether it pays off in the long run depend on many variables. If the child's mythmaking is creating a strained relationship, perhaps you'd better begin to confront the situation and talk over some positive approaches. If fairy tales about the absent parent don't burn themselves out but instead become magnified and flourishing, they can be a destructive force in the relationship between all of you. Stepparents and professionals described both ends of the fantasy spectrum to us—those that are harmless and those that cause untold mischief.

One psychologist recounted the turmoil that occurred in a family close to her. Nine years ago two little girls, five and seven, were left without a mother when she committed suicide. Their father remarried someone he deeply loved and who showed promise of being a good stepmother. The five-year-old had only a vague recollection of her mother but wasn't aware that she had killed herself. The older girl not only knew about the suicide but had been perceptive and mature enough to know that life between her natural mother and father had not been without its problems. This father, filled with guilt about the way his first wife died, couldn't bring himself to talk to his children about it. He wanted to shut it from his mind, live a new, happy life with his present wife, and carry forward. The younger daughter, in fact, had many of the same qualities as her mother, and this made it even more difficult for him to discuss her mother with her—or even to try to discipline her. So the little one grew up as daddy's little girl, getting discipline from no one except her stepmother. Near the end of grammar school, she started to hunt up pictures of her mother and began to make a shrine out of her room. She thought of her mother as a beautiful lady, sweet and loving. When she reached the teen years, she became more and more difficult to handle, and the relationship with her stepmother became increasingly strained. After all the years of trying to raise a little girl whose shadow mother competed with her, the stepmother finally got her husband to sit down and tell the girl some truths. One session with his daughter was not enough, but it was a start toward her facing facts and coming to realistic terms about her mother—and her stepmother.

Another girl who fantasized about her natural mother did not do so out of ignorance of the facts but because she needed to rewrite history. Her mother had been a drug addict, and the daughter had fled from her to the safety of her father's house. She refused to have anything to do with her mother during her final, tormented years, and when the sick and debilitated woman died, the daughter expressed no outward signs of grief. But when she prepared for her own marriage, there was a sudden turnabout. Her fiance's mother had a lingering, progressive illness and was constantly being hospitalized. Yet her warm and generous family spent every available moment caring for her. It was more than the girl could bear, remembering how she had "rejected" her own sick mother. "All of a sudden," related her father, "this girl who had been so happy and loving with her stepmother became cold and indifferent. Pictures of her mother appeared on her walls, she complained that she had really had a miserable time all the years of living with her stepmother and me, that we had snatched her away from her mother, and that she had been constantly unhappy because of this. She told the same story to her fiance's family. She was safe creating the myth because her mother had died, and there was no longer the reality of a drugged mother in the background. I have no idea when, if ever, she will come to terms with the myth she's created. She has wrecked her relationship with her stepmother, although oddly, most of her tastes, how she cooks and dresses, come from her stepmother. Yet I can't blame my wife for feeling that this is pretty poor payment for all the years of love and guidance that she gave my daughter."

Should he tear down the fantasy in front of his daughter's husband? He's afraid to, realizing that if she needs a crutch this badly, she is in deep emotional trouble. Since she actually does know the truth, he can't help her by pushing it on her. She'll have to come around on her own, if she can.

Some children of divorce who infrequently see their absent parent can develop strong fictions about what he or she is like. Beyond that, they may depend so much on their memory that they romanticize what it had been like. Dave, a stepfather, recalled that for five years he thought he and his stepdaughter had been very close. Since they lived far away from her natural father, Dave had become the confidant, disciplinarian, surrogate. But once the girl reached her early teens, she talked more and more about things she remembered, or thought she remembered, about her father. But she mixed him up so much with her stepfather that she had trouble differentiating who had promised what, who had forgotten what, who had disappointed her, who had given her things. The stepfather was baffled and could have become angrier except that he and his wife decided it was time to get myth separated from fact. "I was sure," said the girl's mother, "that things were going to get worse and worse if she didn't get to know her father and find out his bad qualities as well as his good qualities. It wasn't fair to any of us, including her, to idealize a fantasy father. So I suggested she live with him for as long as she wanted—until she's on her own, if that's the way it works out. It was the right move. I think his halo has slipped a little bit, and she is beginning to remember who promised what and who delivered what. Aside from that, I think it's a very natural step in her growing. She should know him as a human being—not as a fictitious white knight."

Some children admit that while they appear to mythologize the absent parent, it isn't to the degree that some stepparents believe. Most children are realistic deep down about what to expect from a parent. "I know my own mother pretty well even though I don't live with her," said a college student. "But I also know that my stepmother thinks I worship the ground my mother walks on, that I believe everything my mother tells me, and that I think she's the most generous, intelligent person in the world. That's a crock. But if I talk about her accomplishments—and she does have a few—my stepmother freezes up. Even my father thinks I've put her on a pedestal, but that's not a fact. If I had to go to anyone for advice, I wouldn't go to her. I know her biases and failings, but I'm too loyal to talk about them. So here we are, and they think I've built up fantasies about her that somehow should be knocked down. It's ridiculous."

This stepdaughter is not dumb. She's emotionally stable, and she isn't causing problems with her father and stepmother by her loyalty to her absent mother. If myths, however, pervade your stepchild's perception to the point that there's trouble afoot, then a useful approach would be to encourage the child to live with or have lengthy visitation with the absent parent so that the myths can be faced. If that's not possible, then some real-life truths should be offered by your mate.

But professionals are unanimous in this: Be careful, be careful. The absent parent must not be diminished to the level of expendable trash. The results should not be greater than to help the child come out of the clouds to the point his psyche can bear.

What About Manipulation and Discrimination by In-laws?

"As much as I love my own mother, I had to recognize that she was a divisive influence with my stepchildren; she was really a disaster."—a stepfather.

"I like my stepgrandmother. I see her only occasionally, but I feel at ease with her."—a stepdaughter.

No one can really be neutral about in-laws. Their very existence represents an influence on at least one member of the family, and they serve to widen not only the family ties but the family conflicts too. In a stepfamily, where feelings of loyalty, rejection, and resentment are heightened anyway, in-laws with an ax to grind can be terrors of destruction, and in-laws with a special sensitivity can be welcome havens of support.

It is the manipulative in-law that can create the greatest amount of chaos, because the children are often unaware of what is actually happening. Manipulation, by its very nature, is stealthy, and most children aren't old enough or sophisticated enough to comprehend what is going on. Where a grandparent discriminates between a stepgrandchild and a natural grandchild, the stepgrandchild generally knows what is going on and can feel the discrimination. But this is not so with the manipulated child, who may react in a way to suit the grandparent, yet not realize it until much later.

Why do grandparents manipulate and discriminate? They might want to gain or retain power over the grandchildren or their parents, power to call the shots for whatever purpose they deem appropriate. They might be fearful of being overlooked, of being ignored, and so they strive to make their presence felt. They might want to express their disapproval of their child's new family in the strongest possible way or exert a primary claim to their natural grandchildren. They could even be hoping to break the new marriage apart.

A classic instance of attempted manipulation happened to Charles, a young social worker. Charles's wife had two little boys from her first marriage, while Charles had never been married before. Charles knew that his stepson's grandmother—the mother of their natural father—had been a dominant force in the previous marriage and that she wanted to continue her dominance over the lives of the two little boys. Charles knew he would have to confront this sooner or later if he wanted to have respect and credibility in his own home. The opportunity came quickly. "Not long after we were married," he recalled, "the grandmother called me on the phone and started telling me about my wife's relationship to their son, about the difficulties they all had had with her behavior. The criticism was lengthy and heavy, and I listened to all she had to say."

Charles had been told by his wife even before they were married that he shouldn't get involved in the relationship between the boys and their grandmother, that the grandmother was an important person in the boys' lives and was happy to take them for extended visits. "So I didn't say anything for a while. But then this woman started telling me about the psychological ramifications of my wife's alleged behavior, and I could see what she was up to." Charles didn't do anything about it then, but he related the conversation to his wife. A few days later the grandmother called back again, and Charles was ready for her. "I did one simple thing. I went over what she had told me and then asked her, 'What do you want me to do with this information? What was your purpose in telling me?' She answered that because I was a social worker, I should know all these things so I could be able to understand my wife better. I said, 'I do know what's going on, and your perceptions and my perceptions are much different. Now, what do you want me to do with the information?' Well, she had no way to answer that because of course all she wanted to do was cause trouble."

Since that time the grandmother has left Charles and his family alone except to call and inquire about the children. "She knew she was in a poor position to exert control," Charles said, "because I refused to play her game and argue back. She could have probably outscreamed and outyelled anyone, but if she had to explain her own behavior, her only response could be, 'I'm only trying to tell you what's best,' and the way you handle that is the answer, 'How do you know what's best?' "

The grandparent who discriminates in favor of his or her natural grandchildren can make the stepgrandchildren feel the rejection heavily. This is especially true where the other members of the family—the natural parent and stepparent—have worked hard to relate to the children on an equal basis, to eliminate as much as possible the "your, mine, ours" philosophy. Not only will the stepgrandchildren react unfavorably, but the parent whose children are being shunted aside is bound to resent it as well. One stepmother recalled the inequities her own two children suffered. "When we were first married, my in-laws had a party for my husband's birthday, and everyone was invited except my two children. That was especially cruel because his children were about the same age. I know my father-in-law was behind this, and my husband was embarrassed when my older daughter asked why she couldn't come. All he could say was, 'You weren't invited.' It didn't help my daughters much."

Stepchildren who bear the onus of the discrimination often hope their parents or stepparent can make things right. But to some stepparents it's perfectly natural for grandparents to be distant with their stepgrandchildren, and they don't see the discrimination for what it is.

This is what happened with Harvey and his mother and his three stepchildren. In the first place Harvey had married a European, and that didn't sit well. Then, Harvey really didn't pay much attention to the way his mother treated the stepgrandchildren. "My mother never approved of my marriage, and she never accepted the kids. On the surface she appeared to be a kindly grandmother, but actually she was overly critical of the children and their mother."

Harvey's mother had two natural grandchildren, and she lavished all her praise and attention on them. When his stepchildren would complain to him, Harvey would tell them they were imagining things, that she really wasn't going out of her way to be nasty to them. But Harvey's oldest stepdaughter thought otherwise. "My stepgrandmother blamed us for everything," she said, "and we got no support from my stepfather or mother. It's very hard if your parents don't see your side."

The stepchildren had only each other for understanding, and they tried to fathom the way their stepgrandmother treated them and the fact they got no help from their mother or stepfather. It left them sad and bewildered. "It's terrible when people you count on don't realize when a kid is suffering because of an evil or nasty relative," Harvey's stepdaughter added. "There's very little you can say to the person who is acting unfairly. They won't change or even admit they are being unfair."

Finally, Harvey saw the light and offered to move his family a few hundred miles away. The stepchildren and their mother jumped at the chance, and now they are all free of the stepgrandmother's open and calculated favoritism.

Harvey offered one certain answer to the discriminatory or manipulating in-law, but you may not need to go so far. You can reduce contact between the grandparent and the children or parent by limiting telephone calls, visits, even meetings. Make sure you and your mate know what is going on and be prepared to speak to the grandparent about it directly. Once you sense there is some discrimination or manipulation, encourage your children and stepchildren to talk to you about it.

But where nothing seems to work, where you know that rank discrimination will only bring unhappiness to your children or stepchildren, it may be time to end the relationship altogether. "When the situation is distressful," says psychiatrist Willem Bosma, "I've recommended the relationship be terminated. Some grandparents can be very cruel."

Bosma's approach is seconded by psychologist Frank Strange,

though he adds a caution. "First, be sure you and your mate perceive manipulation and discrimination the same way, and then decide you are going to confront the grandparents with what you have observed. Next, see if the grandparents observed it the same way. If so, but they feel their actions were justified, and you don't feel they were justified, all you really can do is terminate the relationship, though you must recognize that you may only be terminating the visitation of the stepgrandchildren but not of the natural grandchildren."

No one, however, should speak lightly of ending a relationship, especially where one or more people in the stepfamily have a biological tie with the grandparents. To end the relationship for some and not for others will undoubtedly bring resentment, but sometimes this too is preferable to continuing in a more destructive vein. "I hate to say that terminating a relationship may be the best alternative, because I'm all for working out the problems in the whole family setting," concludes Dr. Strange. "I try to be cautious and not get into dead ends like that, but truly there are some relationships that are so detrimental that the best course is just to put an end to it."

Holidays and Other Special Events

The celebration of holidays is a reflection of individual cultures, but fortunately most of us are not so tradition minded that we can't be flexible. This applies especially to stepparents. Yet sharing holidays and birthdays with the children of split parents is a nagging reminder that the family that existed before you came into the picture still exists in a modified form.

Planning for holidays is not simple. It cuts through legal and emotional divisions, stirs up enmity, jealousy, and fear, and has the potential for making one feel like an outsider. But by using good sense and good humor you can make things better for everyone.

If the court has ruled that visiting stepchildren are limited to "every other Christmas" or "every other spring vacation" or "three weeks in the summer," and your counterpart is tough and demanding, then ease up on asking for anything special such as having the kids on their birthdays. It's not worth the grief. You can make up for those lost birthdays in other ways, by having parties or special trips to celebrate at another time. When one father wistfully commented that it had been nine years since he had spent a birthday with either of his sons, his second wife nodded, but not sympathetically. She reminded him that in those past nine years she had held nine nonbirthday parties for the boys. Gifts had been exchanged, cakes baked, games played, pictures taken. The boys talked most often about the nonbirthday parties put on by their dad and stepmother, because in those nine years their natural mother gave only one of them a party.

"There's so much of this 'I want to get mine' going on between split parents," says psychiatrist Hans Huessey. It's a devilish thing when it happens, and a relatively noninvolved adult is in a good position to counteract it, to become a leveling influence. It's your opportunity to speak up for the child. If you think your mate is unfair in either restrictions or demands, caught up in the "I want to get mine" syndrome, it doesn't hurt to point this out. In fact, the more reasonable you are, the more the feuding pair may come to terms.

Visitation at Christmas may not be the best thing, especially if the child's primary residence is a distance from yours. Have you considered the school, community, scouting, and neighborhood events he may miss by a trip to your town? Have you talked to him or his parent about spending other holidays with you, such as spring vacation or winter break or more of the summer? Dr. Huessey says, "If you sense that the child wants to stay in his home environment where so many things are going on during Christmas vacation, then you should seriously consider leaving him there. I think major holidays should be spent in the primary home."

But there are alternatives to having your visiting stepchild remain in his hometown over school vacation. You can plan special trips for the holidays. Winter trips to ski country or on a sailing charter will be remembered forever. If you and your mate must share a small apartment with your visiting stepchildren, then give serious thought to exchanging your apartment for a house in another part of the country. Even if you can't work out an exchange, friends or friends of friends may want to take a trip themselves and might be willing to turn their house over to you. Some part-time stepfamilies plan their holidays and vacations this way; they and the kids see a new part of the country, look up all the nearby activities, and put in a good week or longer building a common experience that will be a bond forever. One couple arranges fly-and-camp trips. They actively search out people in the southern United States who will rent them a camper for a winter trip. They fly to the city, stock up, and head for the hills. Another stepfamily whose kids are older charter a boat at the end of their flight.

If you can talk over holiday expectations and alternatives, you'll be better off. You may be surprised to find that when you do talk about them, a host of traditional habit patterns will spring forth. Psychologist Frank Strange reminds us that it is not easy to discuss how you are going to handle holidays or visitation or birthdays. "One person might say, 'Well, we should open presents on Christmas Eve,' and another person might say, 'What do you mean? It should be Christmas Day.' What are the expectations that are hidden? How much money should we spend for presents, for instance? Is it a sign that you don't care about someone if you don't make a handmade gift? How are you going to handle gift buying with the children? Do we expect them to exemplify our values? Are they different from the other parent's? I think these are good places to let values come to the surface."

Holidays can be some of the best memories from childhood, and sharing them with step or half sisters and brothers is much of the fun. Most of the professionals agree that if you can work it out among the adults, then the kids ought to get together for at least part of the holiday. Even if there's a large age difference, sharing holidays gives them a bond they can recall. This is not to say that special events shouldn't be planned to accommodate a certain age, like mountain climbing with the older ones and simple camping with the younger. But let them also spend time as a family of brothers and sisters, even if it means giving up some valuable visitation. You'll come out better for it.

4
CONFLICTS

Playing You Off Against One Another

Manipulation seems to be endemic to step relationships. It can take many forms, it can be done with varying degrees of sophistication, and its causes are not usually clear-cut. Understanding the reasons, of course, can be helpful, but even if you just recognize what the child is trying to do, you've taken the first step toward dealing with it.

Parents are frequently myopic about their own children. They imbue them with irreproachable motives and angelic sensitivities. As a stepparent, you are probably more objective and consequently see the children differently.

Some professionals say flatly that all children, in fact all people, are manipulative to some degree, and children learn their special techniques from their parents. But children in stress situations, such as a step relationship, are much more prone to use manipulative techniques. If it pays off, if, through the use of certain behavior, statements, or attitudes, they elicit a Pavlovian response from you or from their natural parent, then you're on the hook.

The methods vary, but the end result is pretty much the same—self-gratification for the child. Sometimes the self-gratification comes from making a parent or his or her mate angry, sometimes from getting either negative or positive attention, sometimes it comes in the form of gifts.

The more common forms of manipulative behavior are:

- choosing stories to suit each adult; the child learns quickly how to pick out that particular item that will get a person stirred up.

- flattery
- tale telling; these are related "informationally," with real or feigned innocence
- whining and teasing
- exacerbating a parent's guilt for the separation or death that broke the family apart
- challenging or arguing to avoid chores
- overt trouble making designed to threaten the new marriage

One Long Island stepmother related how her three stepchildren acted in the first year of extended visiting. "I expected cooperation but didn't get it. They were foot draggers, used to living in a disorderly house. It wasn't long before they started trying to get back at me through their seemingly innocent discussions of what life with their mother was like. For instance, they would tell their mother things that I would do, such as not letting them come in with muddy boots. Then they would tell me her comments about what I did or what I required them to do. 'Mom lets us do it this way' or 'She says we can do it that way' or 'Mom says you're not right.' I didn't waste much sympathy on their being caught in the middle, so to speak. I felt a game was being played, and their father was onto them just as fast. We both talked to their mother and told her what was going on. I don't think she realized the kids had created a running battle between her and me. From that time on, she stopped commenting back. Then the boy tested me about household chores, saying, 'You're the mother, that's your job.' I got the girls aside and said 'Do you see what he's trying to do? Relegate women to a certain role?' We put an end to that cute little technique by ganging up on him and calling him a male chauvinist. That started lots of discussions, and we sorted out how much he really believed and how much was the lazy boy's way of avoiding work. If I had let him get me angry, he would clearly have had the upper hand. I just didn't let him get away with it."

Flattery, however, can be a more effective manipulative tool. Why do we fall for it when deep down we probably know better? If *I* know I'm not the best cook in the world, then why do I believe it when my stepson says I am in order to ease me into laying out a feast for his gang? "You're so understanding" is another gambit. "My mother gets so stupidly angry if I'm not in by the stroke of ten. And she doesn't believe me when I tell her the truth." Doesn't that sound sweet to our ears? Is the snow so thick we can't see what kind of job he's doing?

Sometimes the flattery is aimed at the natural parent, and you are on the sidelines. As a stepfather, you've given a tough order—your stepdaughter's school report for the month showed she missed fifteen of twenty classes, there were no excuses for the absences, and you are angry about the fact that she's sneaking away from school and not doing her assignments. You tell her she's grounded for every day she misses school, and you'll check her out. Then she goes to her mother, tells her the school records are wrong, the computer broke down. She tells her mother that she feels like she's her best friend, and if she had problems, she'd be the first person the girl would confide in.

A stepfather who faced this situation reflected, "It did me no good to pursue my conviction that she must face the consequences for her acts. She had manipulated her mother into being her total ally. Looking back, I can say that if you don't have good communication with your mate, then in a case like this, the best thing you—as a stepparent—can do is back off from confrontation. Kids have an uncanny sense about when things are not meshing between you and your mate, and they soon begin to get caught up in the general manipulation. This time I'm sure my stepdaughter's flattery was all it took to make her mother think she had an ally against me. If they're into that kind of manipulation, then the only alternative I see is to detach yourself, because a relationship exists between the mother and child or father and child that excludes you and can be very destructive toward you. For your own peace of mind and even self-preservation you're better off stepping aside."

Tale telling was almost a ritual among another woman's two stepchildren. They moved in with her shortly after the wedding but would visit their mother from time to time. "They constantly brought back stories about her, her stupidities, her affairs, all the petty things she had done that they didn't care for, all the things people said about her. Maybe they thought they could curry my favor. But I didn't want to get involved with hearing stories about their mother, and when they started to tell them to their father and me, I got busy in another part of the house. I felt it was a touchy subject, so I instinctively wanted to stay out of it. Then, too, I didn't want to get into a position where everything *I* said was being repeated. Unknowingly, though, I let them manipulate me in another way. I insisted that they should write their mother and reminded them twice, three times a week. They'd say okay, but nothing came of it, unless I sat them down and made them write short notes. Finally I asked myself what I was trying to do. They obviously didn't want to write to her but didn't mind my constant reminders. I backed off and thought, 'What am I doing, pushing them into something they hate doing?' I finally realized that with all their tale telling they had made me assume the role of super-lady, and I was going down the line true to form. So I stopped that pretty quickly."

A psychiatrist who is also a stepfather said he noticed that his stepdaughter got what she wanted by using what he termed passive-aggressive behavior. She would wheedle, cajole, fret, and whine until she got whatever treats she wanted. "Not from me, she didn't. However, I recognized that it was the same kind of behavior her mother had used on her first husband and frequently tried with me. The daughter was being manipulative in the same way. She would squeak a lot until her mother took up her cause, whatever it might be—staying up later, extra ice cream." He came out looking like the bad guy, at least to the child's mother, who didn't realize the habit pattern she had set up for her daughter.

If your mate's child challenges you about work he should be doing, it can get wearying. He may throw out arguments that sound cooked up or silly, or excuses and put-offs that serve to undermine you as an authority figure. He might say, "Dad's got something he wants me to do this afternoon, so I don't think I can do that for you." On the surface a remark like this sounds fairly reasonable. And if you repeat it to his father, or his father overhears it, you can be fairly sure that the father is going to feel a little flattered that the boy is conscientious enough to remember to do that special job he had requested. But what's really happening? The boy is subtly letting you know that you don't rank with his natural parent, and though he'd just love to help you, it's got to be some other time when it's more convenient for him.

Child psychologist Jean Chastain recognizes this attitude as a major problem area in the stepparent-stepchild relationship. "The child has a great difficulty accepting a new partner in lieu of his natural parent. The child carries loyalties to the parent whose place you've 'taken'; he's in a bind and has a great deal of difficulty in accepting you as a parent." Perhaps the fact that you are trying to supplant the young person's other parent is unconsciously making her balk, challenge, or invent reasons for not cooperating with you. If you can take your mate aside privately and tell him or her what you think is happening, then your mate may see the wisdom of all of you talking over chores together, so that there will be no room left for the child to move you about like chess pieces.

Criticism from the Other Family

None of us enjoys being criticized, even if we sense that the purpose behind the criticism is to help us improve ourselves. Our ego and our sense of place make it difficult to accept any of it with equanimity.

Put this all into the context of the inevitably tense step situation, and our reactions are painfully amplified. Tensions, motives, roles—all play a part in the manner in which criticism is voiced, in how the message is carried and by whom, in the way we absorb the message.

Suppose you are a stepmother and you and your husband have custody of your stepchild. Your twelve-year-old stepson returns from a weekend with his mother and tells you that she says your marriage won't last. She says she knows dad has been out late almost every night for a couple of weeks and as soon as dad decides to split, then, she says, the boy will come back to live with her.

Once you fight down your anger—because you know that your marriage is going well—it's time to do some thinking. A quick response, perhaps one that answers criticism with criticism, isn't going to help and might cause problems, because the child may feel duty bound to stand up for his parent. "The first question to ask," says Dr. Brandy Adams, "is, 'How did you find out about the criticism?' And if it's a child who has brought the message, that usually implies that the child at that particular moment has a need to say that. So the purpose of the communication is what will deter-mine your response."

You weigh why your stepson has told you this. Is he trying to play you off against his mother? Does he want something? "If these are the reasons," Adams continues, "then the best response is a nonresponse or some general comment such as, 'Everybody's entitled to their opinion,' something very mild and watered down."

Or is this really troubling your stepson, does he feel threatened by it? "If that's the reason, then I think you have to answer and give a full explanation," says Adams. "You might say, 'It's true dad has been out at night a lot, but he's working overtime because we have some big expenses right now. I love him, and I trust him, and I don't think it's necessary to worry about his behavior." The worst thing is to let your anger get the best of you. But even if you decide to lash back, you should try to anticipate the reaction of your stepchild and whether you might bring the child's loyalty conflicts into the open.

Marge is a stepmother who has learned to dampen her anger in the face of some harsh criticism from her husband's ex-wife. But it hasn't been easy, and she is especially vulnerable because her unmarried brother lives with them and is apparently gay. She has two teen-aged stepchildren. "When their mother says nasty things about me, I tell the kids that people get bitter, and they say things that aren't true and that they will have to sort out these things for themselves and decide what is real and what isn't."

And, of course, the stepchildren return from visiting their mother relating her comments about Marge's brother and what must be going on in the house. Marge wisely keeps her cool. "But I get very, very angry—though I keep it to myself—when they tell me things their mother says about my family or about their father. But the fact that they don't take the criticism seriously helps me a lot. If they did, I would feel extra bad."

When it's possible to do so, it's best to discuss any response beforehand with your mate, especially where the child takes the criticism seriously and is disturbed about it. According to psychologist Margaret Doren, "The chances are that the stepchild won't really listen to an explanation from the stepparent, and if you try to argue with the stepchild, it just makes matters worse. If you start defending yourself to the child, then you are making the other parent out to be a liar or at least a disreputable person, and you're doing it in the child's face." She feels that it's most likely the child would jump to her parent's defense, and in fact we know from personal experience that this is invariably the case. Loyalty to his natural parent remains a primary motivation for a child, and a direct attack on that loyalty will only sour whatever relationship you, the stepparent, may have developed. But that doesn't mean that the criticism should be ignored. Your mate might be able to set it straight directly with the child or perhaps through an older brother or sister. As for the stepparent, however, it's best to let your actions speak louder than your words. Or, as Dr. Doren says, "Generally, you're going to offset those untruths with your own behavior."

Sometimes it isn't so easy to learn this. One stepmother felt the competition with the natural parent severely enough when her stepchildren were only visitors. But then she and her husband filed a custody suit and obtained custody of the three older stepchildren. This made her suspicious and oversensitive whenever the children would report anything their mother said. "After we got custody, the children lived about five hundred miles from their mother. They would talk to her on the phone, and we couldn't wait to ask, 'What did she say, why can't she do so-and-so?' Then, we'd get upset when they told us." It took quite awhile before they came to terms with the situation. "We hadn't realized that as little kids, they would probably screw up much of what she said, and then we'd blame her and the kids. Oh, it was a mess, going through a third person like that."

So this stepmother decided to deal directly with her counterpart. "While we were still living so far away from her, she wrote letters to the children and made cutting remarks about me. Then, she sent her baby daughter for a visit with only three diapers, and she wasn't even toilet trained!" The stepmother sat back and began to sort out her feelings. She decided that there was no point in looking for revenge, that she should try to develop a straightforward relationship. "So I began to write to her directly and tell her when something made me angry or I didn't like something she had done or said, or that she hurt me when she made those comments to the children. For a long time she never responded to my letters. But finally she realized I didn't want to hurt her, that I didn't want to replace her as the children's mother. Then, she came to me and asked that bygones be bygones. I guess her need to have me as a friend was greater than her need to stay angry."

There are, then, several possible responses to criticism from your stepchild's natural parent. Depending on what you perceive to be the child's motivation for informing you, or on whether the information comes from your mate or directly from the other parent, you can—

- make an innocuous response, indicating you don't believe the criticism justifies anything stronger
- respond with a full, unalloyed explanation of why the criticism isn't truthful or appropriate
- show your anger when you know it isn't going to result in loyalty conflicts for the child
- contact the other parent directly to clear the air
- enlist the aid of your mate in any response
- demonstrate by your behavior that the criticism doesn't apply

In addition, one stepfather and one stepmother found still another way of dealing with this criticism—they ignored it.

- *stepfather:* "The children's father said that one of the girls had told him I made her sit in a chair for two hours because she 'missed her father.' I made no response to that. I wouldn't dignify such a ridiculous statement."
- *stepmother:* "The boys' mother was one of those who tried to cause trouble, but I suppose I'm not that easy to stir up. I just disregarded most of her slander. I've lived here all my life, and people know me. I'm sure they disregard it too."

Suppose Your Mate and Stepchild Argue?

Hostility between a parent and a child is not uncommon, especially when the two have been separated because of a divorce. Absence does not seem to make the heart grow fonder. Absence alienates, creates unreal expectations, encourages mythmaking. A father, for instance, whose teen-age son comes to live with him for the first time in five years is going to be in for a shock. So will his son. Both remember the other from contact during visitation, and this is nothing like living together. Hostilities are almost destined to show up sooner or later.

But often there is a role for the parent's mate when hostilities erupt, and both the children and the natural parents who spoke with us were quite emphatic about this.

Many boys start to live with their father when they reach their teens, especially if their father has remarried. And it's a rare relationship that doesn't experience stress. One stepmother recalled the petty bickering between her husband and her stepson that began within two weeks after the boy moved in with them. "They were at loggerheads with each other, both trying to butt at each other. At first I thought they could work it out, that it would run down of its own weight. But then it seemed as if they were compelled to thrash things out. My husband, I realized, was suddenly confronted with this tall young man who had a personality of his own and a physique to rival his father's. Of course, he had 'seen' him grow up, but he hadn't lived with the growing up, not for five years!"

Many people would be tempted to jump in and tell them both to knock it off. This stepmother was tempted too. During some superficial conflicts, she tried to voice her opinion, but it seemed to resolve nothing. "I saw myself in the role of mediator. But then I know I couldn't be a mediator in the midst of conflict. Although some of the fights seemed stupid, they represented great tensions between father and son. The boy wasn't ready to be governed, he hadn't been for five years. You don't govern much when you're an absentee parent. I decided not to enter into the battle but took them aside separately to explain what I saw happening and what I thought they were doing. For instance, I'd say to my husband, 'You're arguing on a teen-age level, you want him to listen to the kind of music you like, you put down his reading tastes, his music tastes, his silly stories. You try to make him toe the line as if he were ten years old. You've got to realize he's trying to become a man, and he's getting close to the time when he will be.' Then I would take my stepson aside and say, 'Look, it's not that easy for your father. You're a whole new person, and we're having to adjust to you, but you will have to be more respectful. You can't go around belittling his opinions and criticizing him. You've got to be even more courteous and polite to him than you feel you need to be.' "

Her words had an effect. Her stepson now appreciates that someone could see what was going on, and he and his father have now
stopped squaring off.

Another stepchild said that the most important role her father's
second wife had was to help him understand the things that made her
angry. Looking back on her relationship with her stepmother, Susan
recalled that she wasn't fond of her in the beginning because she
seemed like an assertive person, someone who would push her father
around, and quite unlike her mother. But Susan and her father began
to have open battles after the divorce. He would take out the anger
he felt toward his ex-wife on his daughter, undoubtedly because
Susan still lived with her mother and stoutly took her part. Susan
had worked in her father's motel from the time she was twelve, helping out in the kitchen, running errands. At sixteen, after the divorce,
she worked full time in the summer, and that's when the trouble
really started. "Every time we fought, he'd bring my mother into the
picture. Once, it was particularly nasty, and I walked out of the res-
taurant and went to talk to my stepmother. I told her how I felt
about everything, that he should stop picking on me and bringing
my mother into it. She jumped right in and helped me out. That was
the first time she patched things up, talking to him and explaining
that it wasn't right to keep scolding about my mother because that
had nothing to do with our disagreement. She made him realize he
shouldn't do it. He's still hard to get close to, and he still fights with
me, but my stepmother talks to him, and then she'll talk to me and
explain why he feels bitter about something. She speaks up to him
about me and helps me forgive and understand him. If she didn't do
this, maybe my father and I would just stop seeing each other."

It is easy to be drawn into a fight. You look at the fuming child
and say, "I don't want to hear you talk like that to your mother." Or
you give vent to your frustrations: "I'm glad you're not mine because
I wouldn't put up with that for one moment." But hold off. What is
really going on between parent and child? And should you become a
part of it? It's one thing to observe and evaluate the hostilities and
then help; it's quite another thing to get caught up in the power
struggle and sound off. You'll find yourself in a no-win position
again because whatever is going on between those two is not your
immediate business, unless it looks as if things could get violent.
Step back and wait until tempers cool before you help. If you find

yourself getting into the fray, the hostilities may soon center on you. One Pennsylvania stepmother caught herself in this kind of involvement. "One time my two stepchildren and their father got into a nasty argument. They were starting to dredge up things about the divorce, and I entered into it trying to get the record straight. Soon I realized that while they were talking *about* me, the hostility really was their problem. It was between *them*. I said, 'Hey, now, this has nothing to do with me, does it? It's really between you and your father, isn't it?' and the kids tearily said, 'Yes.' So I got out of there."

Stepfathers often see hostility between mother and teen-age daughters, and many have felt compelled to take the mother's part, especially when the daughter gets cutting and abusive. It's tough not to. Our culture seems to demand that men come to their wife's defense. But while doing so may make your wife feel better, it won't get at the underlying cause of your teen-age stepdaughter's anger. Sometimes the teen-ager becomes passively aggressive toward her mother, subtly letting her know that she has angers.

One girl visited her mother and stepfather every other weekend, arriving on a Friday and leaving on Sunday evening. Her mother was particularly lonely without her and insisted that she visit at least that often. But the daughter harbored deep angers about her mother's divorce that she had managed to cover up, at least on the surface. Every weekend visit she would come loaded with books, and after a perfunctory sharing of a meal, she'd take to her room to study, that night, all the next day, and all the day after, most of the time busying herself with work that wasn't due for days, even weeks ahead. It became apparent to the stepfather that she was plainly saying to her mother, "You can insist that I visit, and so I'm here, but I resent it, and I resent you." The stepfather wisely stepped into the picture because the girl was succeeding in punishing everyone. His wife was miserable and bewildered, and her daughter quietly determined not to involve herself on any positive level with either of them. He took his wife aside and told her what he saw happening and suggested that she and her daughter face up to it. He suggested that future visits should be totally left up to the girl, that she should come only when she felt she could spare the time from her books, and if she wanted to bring a friend, well and good. It was hard for this stepfather not to wade in and tell his stepdaughter off. But he was wise enough to realize that what was going on between these two people was confined to them. He was incidental to the situation and must be nothing more than advisor to his wife. His suggestion worked. At first the girl came crying to him, asking him to explain to her mother that she really had all this work to do, but he adamantly refused to be drawn in. It was five weeks before she came back, but when she did, it was without the books. It was also the start of a good friendship between the three of them.

Dr. Brandy Adams, in discussing hostility between parent and child, says it is important to determine the reasons for the hostility. "A certain amount is genuine, and a certain amount is not. It's just a game. It may not be a deliberate, conscious game, but a game nevertheless. A child may have developed it to pit one parent against the other or to gain something. These hostilities have to be dealt with differently than those when the child is merely frustrated or angry. Sometimes you have to deal with hostility by absolutely refusing to acknowledge its existence openly or to return any type of feedback. In other cases you might want to get the child to verbalize it openly, to discuss it. There are even situations when you should openly disapprove of it."

The consensus drawn from both good and bad experiences, however, seems to favor that the stepparent bring objectivity to bear, to steer clear of the direct conflict, and in extreme cases, for self-preservation, to totally withdraw.

Who Comes First— the Children or You?

We're confident that almost any adult who has lived with other people's children has wondered where he or she stands in the family. Do you make sacrifices for the children, only to have them taken as a matter of course? Are you expected to do all the giving? An adult taking on kids for the first time may wonder why the natural parent stands up for the children and not for him? Were the children the main reason you married, would you have married if it hadn't been for the children? And finally, who comes first, you or the children?

The difficult thing is in knowing ahead of time, before you begin living together, if the children are more important than you are. It's doubtful that your mate would admit to it, and the chances are you aren't on the lookout for it anyway. You can easily fool yourself by thinking that these children need you, that you are going to rescue them from growing up in a single-parent family. You will become such an indispensable cog in the household, you tell yourself, that there's no question about who the important one will be.

But you overlook the fact that your mate got along before you came into the picture and doubtless will get along should you leave. The crucial issue is not how important you are to the children but how strong and secure your relationship is with your mate.

"If the stepchildren are the excuse for the marriage," says psychologist Margaret Doren, "then the marriage really hasn't much to go on. It has three strikes against it before it starts. The interpersonal problems in a remarriage are even greater than if it were just two kids getting married for the first time. Establishing a marriage relationship *and* a parent relationship at the same time is extremely difficult because you are adjusting to a whole family relationship, perhaps five, six, or seven new and different people. The problems are squared, not just multiplied."

Cora hadn't worked out her relationship with her husband to the point where she knew where she stood until it really was too late. Her stepdaughter's mother had died when the girl was only two, and for the next three years the girl had lived alone with her father and his mother. "When we married, my five-year-old daughter was in the wedding party, and that was okay. But then she drove across country with us, and I was very upset. I felt I was being deprived of a great deal that I needed—privacy with my husband and a chance to have a honeymoon."

But it didn't stop there. "Everything revolved around my stepdaughter, and whenever she misbehaved, I was blamed for it. All of this made her think she was much more important than she actually was, and I thought she probably needed some counseling. But no one agreed with me. They all thought I was the one who should do the adjusting."

Cora's stepdaughter is now a teen-ager, but the relationship between them is distant, and Cora has stored some resentments toward her husband. "From the beginning he put his daughter first, undoubtedly out of guilt. If you think of marriage as togetherness, then in our case it always was the three of us together, or he and my stepdaughter together. Frankly, I feel I've been victimized."

"The most important thing that makes a stepfamily work," says Dr. Doren, "is for the two adults to love each other enormously. They must put each other first, and then work out the problems with the stepchildren. Whenever the stepchildren are placed first, above the stepparent, the marriage is in trouble."

Professionals advise again and again that if possible, you should work out your expectations, your mate's expectations, even the children's expectations before the marriage. If your mate believes the children should come first, and you feel this isn't proper, you may have no alternative but to end the relationship, unless you feel you can change things once you marry (which, we should point out, is pretty much a vain hope). If your mate is ambivalent about it all, you might be able to convince him or her that what you two mean to each other is far more important than whether your stepchild might have a temper tantrum or be hurt or feel left out. It's quite clear, though, that unless you know from the beginning whether your relationship with your mate is more important than the interests of the stepchildren, you are bound to have big problems.

Grace was one stepmother who thought she had worked these things out only to find that after six months she was back in second place. She and her husband had talked things over before they married, and he had led her to believe that his interest in his three children was not very strong. He was more interested in living with her. "But then my eldest son, who had been living in California with his father, joined us, and that's when things began to go bad." The boy was caught with several ounces of marijuana, and according to Grace, "My husband is simply death on that sort of thing. He kicked the boy out of the house and wouldn't have anything more to do with him." And then Grace's husband started to take an interest in his own children, at the expense of his relationship with Grace. One issue was discipline. "Whatever his boy does is never as bad as what my son may do. They are both typical teen-agers, but when I try to point out how he is protecting his own child, my husband just won't listen." Grace has tried to discipline her other stepchildren as well, but her husband doesn't back anything she does or says. "If I put one of them on restriction for disobeying, and three or four days later they want to go somewhere and I'm not home, my husband just lets them go. Then, when I talk to him about it, he just defends his own kids."

What happened to Grace is an example of fairly common behavior by parents whose children are living with them. Sometimes they try to set themselves between their mate and their own child so they may insulate that child from some imagined harm by their mate. Child psychologist Jean Chastain has seen this frequently, and she thinks it is one of the greatest sources of friction in the stepfamily. "The custodial parent will intervene in inappropriate ways and at inappropriate times to 'protect' the stepchild from the stepparent. When this happens, the problems that arise between stepchild and stepparent never have a chance of being worked out."

Another word for it is "overreaction," and Dr. Brandy Adams thinks it happens most frequently—but not always—in the months immediately after a bitter divorce, when the parent has an overriding need to be protective of the offspring. "The natural parent should stay out of the efforts of a stepparent and stepchild to work out a relationship," he says. "The process of accommodation and interaction should be allowed to go forward unless there is obvious danger or destruction." In his mind the parent who intervenes is really doing two things: telling the child that the parent's mate is not so important after all and telling his or her mate that the parent will be the judge of when he or she crosses the line. We can also add a third effect: hinging the relationship between the two adults, at least partly, on how well the partner gets along with the child.

One of the more difficult areas is money—who's entitled to it and who decides where it goes and how. If you feel you are being deprived because so much is going to the child, or if you and your mate keep sacrificing for the child and your mate thinks that's the way it should continue, then you know who comes first. If there is only so much money to go around and you have postponed that trip or new car or new clothes because the child needed braces, then you shouldn't shrink back when the next request is for an electric guitar. At some point money will be important to the continuing vitality of your relationship with your mate. So you had better know how much you count.

In Doris's case almost twenty years went by before she finally put her foot down and made a claim to some of the family's money. She has three stepsons, and for many years she and her husband scrimped and saved so the boys could have the things their friends had. Now the boys are grown, but money is still going to them. "My husband, out of guilt because he divorced their mother, just forks out thousands of dollars, even after all these years. I finally had to talk to him and say, 'You want me to cut down, not to spend anything, but you go ahead and give them all the money they want.' He said the money was just a loan, and for a while I believed him. But this has been going on for years, so I asked him when he would collect on the 'loans.' Then he said, 'I feel I owe it to them,' and I said, 'Why?' He couldn't really answer that, so I got firm and said, 'You're going to have to collect the money,' and he said he would, and I asked him when, and he said in six months. I told him I'd make it a point to ask about it then."

It wasn't that Doris disliked her stepsons, in fact she enjoyed them. It was just that she had grown tired of coming in second on the money angle, and with the boys grown and on their own, she saw no reason this should continue. In the meantime, however, and probably because the stepchildren have always had a prior claim on the money, Doris and her husband are having difficulties. "This thing about money," Doris says, "has definitely hurt our relationship. Things used to be much more open between us, but not anymore."

The behavioral professionals are much in agreement about who should come first in a marriage or remarriage. Parenting is certainly an important aspect, but it is the relationship between the two adults that takes priority. The most important reason for a love relationship is to gain a mate, not a parent for a child. As psychologist Dana Lehman-Olson pointed out, "Only if a couple's needs are being met through each other have they energy left over for parenting."

What If the Child Has Traits You Dislike?

A stepmother says: "I don't think the way to handle a bad trait in your stepchild is to bring it out into the open and emphasize it."

A stepfather says: "I don't handle unlikable traits in my stepchildren very well. I never bring them out as I should."

These stepparents happen to be married to one another, and all their children happen to live with them. You might expect these mates to share a common approach to the situation, but their very disagreement shows the many and varied responses that can turn up. Having a stepchild with disagreeable traits is not what most of us hoped for, even though, if we had thought a moment, we would have realized that pressures alone in a stepfamily can make for regular unpleasantness. There's anger, guilt, sadness, impatience, resentment, a host of feelings that will precipitate behavior not to your liking. Then, there's the added dimension that when a child with one set of habits and characteristics lives with someone who is not comfortable with those habits and characteristics, the potential for conflict is great. The conflict can more easily erupt, too, because the parent's mate bears no sense of responsibility for the unattractive habits of the child. It wasn't the mate who first raised this child and taught him the things that now seem so unlikable, and it isn't from his or her family that the child's unappealing characteristics spring.

Adults, in spite of their true feelings about their mate's children, frequently go to extreme lengths to mask those feelings, even to themselves. Most of us are caught up with the idea that, somehow, it's just not very nice to have negative feelings about a child, that if we were really *good* parents and good people, we'd know how to rebuff those dark thoughts. For many, many adults it is an extremely difficult thing to finally admit that there are a number of traits in their mate's child that they actively dislike.

In stepfamilies we are dealing with divided loyalties, unfamiliar expectations, and an overriding urge not to rock the boat in the second marriage—in short, it's simply easier to pretend to feel the way we're expected to feel. But actually, loving your stepchild is a more difficult thing than not loving her, and psychiatrist Willem Bosma thinks the latter is more natural too. "It's hard enough for many parents to love their natural children, and in fact many parents will love one child and not the other." It's often understandable, Bosma feels, for an adult to harbor such feelings of dislike. "There are some children who are simply unlovable. Perhaps they fight like hell or are terribly destructive. If you can realize that you don't have feelings of love for this child—for whatever reason—you might be more realistic in the treatment of the child."

Bosma has come across a number of cases where a stepparent was mightily disturbed by dislike for the stepchild. There was a great deal of guilt for not feeling some sort of love. "You try to explain that the child only has one choice," Bosma says, "and that is to live with you. The child will identify with you even if it isn't yours, by the very nature of living with you. So your influence is there, even if you don't have warm feelings for the child. And you shouldn't be hung up by your lack of warm emotion."

One set of circumstances that seems particularly distressing to parents' mates is where the child has a marked physical or emotional resemblance to the absent parent. It's a constant reminder that your partner did live with someone else before you and had sex with that person, which produced this child. This can cause some people to develop an active dislike whenever the child evidences any of the characteristics of the other parent.

One stepfather had particular problems with his teen-aged step-son. The boy had been his father's favorite and greatly resembled the father. "There wasn't any discipline from the father," the stepfather recalled. "The only one he paid any attention to was this boy—and this made the boy think he was special." The stepfather resented the boy's attitude and the fact that he could have been his father's double, a fact neighbors and friends kept pointing out. So he worked up a dislike for the boy and subjected him to some heavy discipline. It was a mistake. "Perhaps I came on too strong, at least I think so now." But instead of letting this dislike eat away at him, the step-father backed off a bit and made himself realize that the boy couldn't help resembling his father and that he wasn't to blame for not being disciplined. The stepfather concluded that he himself would have to do some changing, and now, seven years later, this stepfather has legally adopted the boy.

Most such situations don't end this happily, however. The dislike remains because the resemblance remains, and often with each new, recognizable trait, the dislike grows. It isn't like a dirty window that can be wiped off when it offends you—no one can really change his looks, and when it comes to personal habits, they are much too ingrained.

One of the professionals we spoke with had had a drug-using alcoholic for a first wife and was concerned about his children, most of whom still live with him and their stepmother. His first wife was almost incapable of maintaining anything but a stiff, formal relationship with anyone. "We've underplayed the genetics involved in the children we take on," he said, adding that not much is really known about what weaknesses and strengths are passed from generation to generation. "What troubled my wife most was that her stepchildren had similar types of relationship problems as their natural mother. They too found it difficult to have a relaxed, undemanding friendship with others. At first I thought her feeling was based on the fact that the kids were stepchildren. But then I looked closely at the characteristics she saw and realized that much of what was unappealing in my kids had been passed down from their mother."

Sometimes it isn't just a dislikable trait that a person sees in a child; it's his or her own general dislike of the natural parent, which carries over to the child. In the long run this can only work to deepen bitterness inside the family. One young Iowa mother was having this kind of a problem. "I can't figure out why I don't like Jane any better, but I pass it off that no one particularly likes Jane. I think she's starting to act an awful lot like her mother—jealousy and bossiness especially. Sometimes I wonder if it's the animosity toward her mother that I feel that I direct at Jane. I honestly hate her mother."

There's no reason to feel ashamed or guilty because you don't like certain characteristics in your mate's children. But understand where your feelings come from, whether it's the child you don't care for or the parent. In either event, most of the professionals told us, it's not good to let your feelings fester inside you. It's better to get your feelings out on the table so your mate, at least, can understand how you feel and help you deal with it.

A number of people offered suggestions for dealing with dislikable or unacceptable characteristics:

Talk it out. Sandy married a widower with two young girls. From the first, the girls' grandparents interfered with the way Sandy was trying to raise them. The girls continually treated her as an outsider, often ignoring her questions and directions. "I found that the love I wanted to give these children turned to dislike. I told my husband I was resentful of the girls, his mother and father, and even him, for not standing up for me. Then I told the girls that what they were doing was very upsetting. I expressed my dismay. I felt a lot better, and things straightened out a little after I verbalized my hurt and anger."

Back off, loosen your contact. Marvin, a bachelor, acquired three children when he married. One was in her early teens. There wasn't much discipline in the household, and Marvin tried to take hold. "As soon as my daughter got into high school, she started to change overnight, wearing provocative clothes, skipping classes to hang out with dropouts. I was enraged with her for exhibiting this kind of behavior and associating with people I had no use for. But she turned to her mother to look for sympathy and got it. I became even more angry and shouted, but it did no good. My wife had neutralized me. So I backed off from trying to change my stepdaughter. Eventually she came around without my interference."

Develop a thick skin. Rosa is a school teacher and the stepmother of three children. From her perspective, their manners were poor, and they could be quite mean to one another, including Rosa. She cringed when they went to any public place together. But she persisted in trying to teach them manners. "I hung in there. But I couldn't let my feelings get hurt by everything they did. I think we should avoid taking a child's bad behavior personally, because when they're growing up, they're quite uncivilized. It takes awhile for them to become civilized. If you let your feelings get hurt by every thoughtless thing they do, you're going to be crying all the time. You've got to develop a thick skin."

If all else fails, keep the child away from the house. Marian's oldest stepson was only a dozen years younger than she, but she never felt at ease with him. He was usually in trouble, and there were times when the police were about the house asking questions. Since the boy's father was a salesman and on the road most of the week, he spent a major part of the time with Marian. "But I could never leave him alone and never trusted him to baby-sit because I never knew what the house was going to be used for. He could burn it down around our heads. Then, one weekend he took my car, and he was picked up in a drug raid. They found a list of his customers. He was a juvenile dealer. I finally admitted to myself that I had disliked him from the start and didn't need the grief of having him around anymore. So I told his father to send him back to his mother or make other arrangements. And he did."

Disliking traits in the child of one's mate is neither so unnatural nor so unsavory as to merit the guilt that many people attach to it. As psychiatrist Gordon Livingston points out, "It's perfectly natural not to like one's stepchild. It's also natural to actively dislike him."

Must You Treat Your Children Equally?

Degrees of discrimination between stepchildren and natural children seem to pervade stepfamily relationships.

Dr. Benjamin Spock stated fifteen years ago that not even natural parents can treat two of their own children alike,* so what really can we expect from a stepparent? Since most stepfamilies experience some form of discrimination, what we become concerned with is the degree of that discrimination, why it occurs, and how it affects the family structure.

"My stepfather," said one young woman, "was a harsh disciplinarian, that is, until my sister was born. He always said children should be treated equally, and he managed to do that with us until he had his own child. Then she always got more than we did. I think discipline should be even-handed as he said, but when I tried to discipline her myself, he would criticize me. I think, as far as my stepfather was concerned, this was his child, and she could have anything."

The youngest is usually treated better than the oldest, even within natural families, because of tolerance and experience. Yet an older child may view this as stepparent discrimination. Stepparents who can look objectively at their changed tolerance level often say, "I guess I mellowed." Of course they have. Raising a child from babyhood instead of taking on one that is half-grown is a mellowing experience.

With all the subtle and crude discrimination that goes on in stepfamilies, a surprising number of children do not seem to resent each other. As one young man recalled, even though his halfbrother got to go to summer camp and received an allowance that never did, he did not begrudge it. "I never felt he was getting something that should have been mine. I took care of him and was glad he had a chance to have things better than I did. I think of myself as being the

* *Problems of Parents* (Boston: Houghton Mifflin, 1962), pp. 244–245.

stepson of the turbulent years and my brother the one who came along when things were calmer."

In families where there are two sets of stepchildren, there is a greater chance for rivalry and competition. Sociologist Gerda Schulman points out one common discriminatory technique. There is "an inclination to use one's own children as models and the other parent's children as weapons or targets so that the children are often caught in a current of misuse and exploitation which finally erupts in a free-for-all battle among the children, who find it safer to fight one another than to fight the parental person."*

Yet while the kids may fight with each other, the resentment they feel is aimed at the parent who caused the distress in the first place. Jerry, a college student, recalled a stepmother who used to discriminate against him in this fashion: "She constantly compared me to my stepbrother or stepsister, saying, 'Why can't you be more like them?' or 'Why can't you do this like they can?' Boy, did I hate her doing that. I wanted to tell her, 'I'm myself. You can't change me into something I'm not.' " Her unequal treatment went further than that, however. "My stepbrother recently got out of college and lived here for about four months. At the same time I was working during the summer for college in the fall. She told me I had to pay room and board. I asked her how come my stepbrother didn't have to pay, and she said he was saving for his upcoming marriage. But she's never asked him to pay room and board, and I don't think she ever thought about asking him."

Why hasn't Jerry's father injected himself into the situation to make his wife's treatment of his boy more equitable? In this stepfamily relationship—as in so many others—there is what Gerda Schulman calls a subgroup, and it's usually the basic family. This subgroup is usually accorded the dominant position and sets the style in behavior, manners, and the like. She notes, "The difference in status does not appear to depend on whether the subgroup is headed by the mother or the father . . . but which of the parents is the dominant partner. . . . The communication style between subgroups is usually defensive-aggressive and expressed in such statements as 'My children are better behaved than yours; they have fewer problems; they are more considerate than yours.' "**

*"Myths That Intrude," pp. 135–136.
** Ibid., p. 136.

The actions of Jerry's father bear this out. In fact, he not only deferred to his new wife and her children, but he actively engaged Jerry to follow his lead. Jerry, mystified, could not understand why his father was suddenly a disciplinarian. "After he married my stepmother, he was on my back all the time, asking me to do chores around the house that he never asked my stepmother's children to do. When I asked him why he was picking on me, he denied it. If I forgot to do something, he really yelled at me, although he said nothing to the others."

There are some stepparents who not only recognize that they treat the children unequally but feel they are justified. One couple who had both been widowed before marrying one another produced this exchange:

He: "My greatest irritation is the different treatment the two sets of children receive from my wife."

She: "I admit I treat them differently. I find it very difficult to treat them equally, because his children have had unacceptable behavior. And everything shows with me."

He: "But she should not let superficial behavior determine rank favoritism."

She: I won't treat them equally until they conform to my standards."

He: "I think the children are a vehicle for her to get to me."

We noted that even where inequality of treatment was problably no greater than in natural families, stepchildren perceived that the inequality resulted because there were no blood ties. Fifteen years ago, in fact, an article in *Marriage and Family Living* deduced from replies made by groups of stepchildren that stepparents were believed to discriminate more often than were natural parents, and stepparents of the opposite sex were more often suspected of discrimination than were those of the child's own sex. Stepchildren of both sexes, moreover, believed that stepmothers discriminated more than stepfathers.*

Severe inequality of treatment means rejection and all that the word connotes. This is hard for a child to live with. Yet none of the stepchildren admitted to feeling any inequality when the other child

---

*Charles E. Bowerman and Donald P. Irish, "Some Relationships of Stepchildren to Their Parents," May 1962, p. 120.

was a baby, was sick, or was injured. They sensed that vulnerability requires extra care and attention.

Yet if you bend over backward to be equal right down to the last splash of cola, is that being sensible? One mother who raised her own daughter and a stepdaughter from the time they were two years old regrets that she felt she had to be artificially equal through the years. If they had both been her own, she was sure that on many occasions she would have spent extra effort for one and not the other, would have given the artistic daughter art lessons even if she couldn't have afforded to do something similar for the other. She recalled, "I suppose I was harder on both of them because they were stepsisters. I was terribly conscious of being equal, of trying to keep discipline on the same level. Yet each girl had her own needs and her own level of behavior. I know if I had to do it over again, I would not have tried to be so equal."

One stepparent said he planned to jot down in a book some of the important things he does for the kids and see how it goes after a year. Another says you don't have to do that to know which kid feels he's coming up short. Try asking.

"They Say It Was Better Before I Came on the Scene"

Your mate's children wield a potent weapon when they say to you, "Things were nicer before." We came across several reasons why children might express a desire—subtly or overtly—to return to the good old days before the parent's mate became part of the scene.

- The child had to move to a new neighborhood and give up his old school and friends.
- The child wishes her original set of parents were back together again.
- The child wishes he were still living alone with just the one parent, getting full and undivided attention.

- The child, especially the one who is in her teens, is destructive and full of anger, and wishes to break up the relationship.

Moving to a new neighborhood, especially for a young person who has come to rely heavily upon friends, can be a bitter experience. If you couple this with getting a new parent, you have reached a cause and effect that in the child's eyes is cut and dried. "If you hadn't come along," so the reasoning goes, "I would still have my friends, my school, all the things I'm used to." One stepfather, whose marriage required a move of only forty miles, was in a dilemma. "Sally was so unhappy and sullen that we were tempted to have her board with friends for the next school year instead of coming with us. But then I realized that she had not had a father in the house since she was a baby, and I felt she needed that more than she needed friends at this point. I insisted she move with us, introduced her to all the nice young people I know in the area and just rode out the storm. I'm sure if we had stayed in *her* hometown, things would have been great between us. Instead we had a pretty bad time of it, very tense. She let me know that she had had a better life before her mother and I married. She felt I had done her a personal injustice. But as she started to make new friends, the nastiness subsided. There was no way I could fight her unhappiness. I knew why she was angry, and it was just a question of time."

Little children caught up in a new living arrangement can be just as angry as older children. Psychologists tell us again and again that children in the early years will verbalize dissatisfaction at the way things are. They often speak outright, making uncomplimentary remarks, such as, "I don't like you, I don't want you around, I want my mother and father together again." The temptation to retort in kind is overwhelming. One psychologist who is also a stepfather and who went through this devastating experience with two very young stepchildren said, "I knew what to expect, but of course it still comes as a shock. But I followed my own professional knowledge. I did not let them know they had upset me. I never gave them an opportunity to see they might have me under control by telling me they preferred things the way they used to be. There would have been no adequate answer. They simply had to live through the change."

If this stepfather had responded with an angry retort or wounded feelings, the battle lines might have been drawn, and hostilities might have continued. The children's hopes to get their parents back together again went on for more than a year, until summer vacation, when they spent a month with their father and his new wife. When they came back to their mother and stepfather, they apparently had concluded that both their mother and father's new relationships were permanent, and they themselves would have to make the adjustment. No amount of wishing would make things return to the way they had been.

A young person who has been living with one parent for any length of time brings an extra problem to any new mate of that parent. Imagine all the catering and undivided attention that young person has received. If he's an only child, the difficulty is compounded, because the fear of being an outsider to the new twosome looms even larger.

You might expect to see some reversion to infantile behavior or sudden uncontrollable rage. Even if the parent and child didn't seem to be getting along that well while they were alone together, there is probably a mutual dependency that makes it extra hard on you. You may find the child making absolutely sure that you know you're not the parent. That's fear and jealousy talking. Even if you know this kid has reasons to want to see you on the moon, it's not easy to swallow. Another stepfather recalls, "I knew I would be resented and my stepson would like to throw me out because I was, after all, a major intrusion in their lives. For three years he had lived alone with his mother and had her full attention. He came to believe it would continue this way. So even before our marriage and afterward, we made major efforts to spend time with him, and I let them continue their old pattern of gossiping at bedtime. My wife and I did not take any time away from her son just for the sake of being together during those first couple of months. He still said he wished things were the way they used to be. My answer was, 'Yes, I can understand that. But your mother and I are together. We'll probably be together for a long time.' That's all I would say. Then I gradually eased into his life by doing positive things alone with him—took him to the office with me, got him involved in the part of my life he hadn't known."

Yet some stepfamilies are faced with truly big problems when there's a child who brings deep angers into the home. Margaret Doren, in her psychological counseling, has often observed the bitterness some teen-agers take from one broken marriage to the new relationship. There is almost no accounting for some of the vilification, disrespect, and treachery that stepparents of such children receive. Dr. Doren remarks, "It is so bad that I say to people caught up in an unhappy marriage, 'If you're going to get divorced, do it before the kids are ten years old.' It may be because they are so disillusioned that they carry such angers to the new marriage." Whatever the reasons, everyone caught up in such a predicament needs help. These children cannot bear to see the relationship succeed. If they are emotionally damaged, their need for your destruction knows no bounds. Unless the child's parent is willing to find professional therapy, there seems little one can do.

Often it's only one child in the family who is so afflicted with anger. One stepmother summarized, "The seventeen-year-old boy is a liar and a conniver, trying to turn everyone against me. He says outright, 'I just hate having you live with us and wish my dad and I were alone again.' The kid has finally gotten to me. I don't know how to stop it, but I figure as soon as he's eighteen, he must leave the house. Until then I'm working a ten-hour day at my job just to stay away from home. His mother never wanted him, and I've bought all his clothes, but he still seems to want to destroy me."

It's hard to be turned aside when you come with outstretched arms hoping for a nice relationship. But whenever the parents' mates realized that the kids weren't really angry at them, just exhibiting hostility because they had been caught in a situation not of their choosing, they were better able to handle the situation, either by themselves or with professional help.

Suppose a Child Thinks a Parent's Mate Is Abusive?

"I didn't complain to my mother about this treatment, because I realized for her to take sides would have just made the situation more unpleasant."—*a stepson talking about his stepfather.*

"I can't blame my mother for not coming to our aid. If she had contradicted him, he would have been upset with her as well as with us."—*a stepdaughter talking about her stepfather.*

The abusive adult, even outside of the Cinderella story, turns up in the nicest of homes. Bad treatment, as children see it, runs the gamut from psychological manipulation to outright corporal punishment. The classic child batterer is, of course, in a category by himself, but all gradations of this behavior face children from time to time.

Perhaps the most useful method of judging bad behavior toward a child is to examine it from the eyes of the beholder. A sensitive, delicately reared child can become absolutely traumatized by a loud, crude authoritarian. On the other hand, a tough resilient youngster will take such treatment in her stride and never consider it "abusive." To the former child, though, this kind of handling is considered cruel and exacting.

The adult who is consistently abusive frequently has never had children of his or her own. This person lacks tolerance of the child's failings or youthful exuberance, is not willing to help the child handle emotional and behavioral difficulties, and is prone to use physical discipline.

Even a subtly abusive adult can cause psychological as well as physical damage. Unfortunately, too many children are left to fend for themselves against such an infinitely more experienced and artful foe, because most natural parents don't want to exacerbate a bad situation by jumping into the middle of it.

A young Utah woman recalled growing up under her stepfather's exacting rule. Janice, her brother, and her sister had lived alone with their mother for years before their stepfather entered the picture. At first she was ecstatic. "From the time I was in first grade, I thought I'd really like a father. I had all these ideas that we'd go fishing and riding. I expected so much." But the actuality didn't turn out that way.

"He was a strict man, dishing out almost nothing but criticism. If you did a job well, he never said how nice it was but would pick out all the flaws—like a white-glove inspection. When I was in high school, I had a three-minute telephone limit; he was very strict about that and would go so far as to hang up the phone when I was in the middle of a sentence. I felt he disciplined on whim, and he hit us all the time. Neither my mother nor my grandparents had ever hit us."

Janice finally learned how to cope with all this, but she had to go through some torment first. "He made us all quite tense, so we tried to stay out of his way. But in seventh grade I came close to a nervous breakdown, and I found out it was because I was bottling everything up inside me. Then I just rebelled, and while it got me in big trouble with him, I felt much better. Standing up to him made all the difference."

The interesting thing is that from this stepfather's point of view, what Janice thought of as abuse, he considered good and proper parenting. He remarked that he considered himself genuinely interested in his stepchildren, that he had spent years trying to train them to become responsible adults. His mistake was in never looking at himself from their point of view. But he came by his authoritarianism honestly.

"When I was a kid, I was raised very sternly, and I still have a great deal of admiration for my father. He used to beat hell out of me every day, come home at night and take a strap to me because, he said, I must've done something bad. As I look back on it, I probably deserved it, because I usually did something bad during the day."

This stepfather's story underscores what behavioral professionals tell us repeatedly—the child who is regularly whipped or punished will end up using the same disciplinary measures on the next generation.

In most instances abusiveness in a parent's mate sours the relationship with the child to the point that almost all contact between them will be severed. It didn't happen in this instance, however, probably because of Janice's forgiving nature and closeness to her mother. "Now when I visit, I get along with him much better. I realize he has an inability to express his affection toward any of us stepchildren and apparently even to others. But all we picked up on when we were growing up was his heavy hand."

From her stepfather's point of view, "I'd say my relationship with my oldest stepdaughter is excellent now, even though we had some knock-down, drag-out fights before she left home."

Another form of bad treatment is emotional—hurting or excluding the child by conduct or words. Otherwise nice people can wield such power over children.

Ruth and Annie lived in New York with their mother and stepfather. Their natural father spent considerable time in Europe and on one of his trips met and subsequently married a Swiss woman. One month after they married, they returned to New York, and the girls went to the airport to meet them. "I was prepared to like my new stepmother," said Ruth. "She had written letters to my sister every week—fantastic letters. A day or two after they returned, I called to see if we could spend the next weekend with them, because we hadn't seen our father in such a long time. She said they wanted to be alone and had other plans for the next few weeks." Not only Ruth but Annie, too, became angry and upset, especially when their father didn't step in to rectify the situation. "All he said was, 'You've got to try to understand.' He wouldn't make her back down." Annie tried to see him alone, asking if she could go on business trips with him, but was never able to make it work out. One excuse or another would come up, and finally their stepmother refused to tell them where he could be reached when he was out of town. Ruth eventually wrote to her father asking *him* to be more understanding about spending time with them. Their stepmother sent them a reply telling them she didn't want to see either of them in her home. "It's been horrible for Annie. This woman couldn't have been crueler if she had broken Annie's arms. But my father can't see how much she's hurt us. When I finally saw him alone, I complained about her treatment, and his only reply was that she never had had children and I should try to see it from her point of view, that she doesn't understand about kids."

Ruth and Annie were luckier than some, because they had their own mother and a considerate stepfather to live with. Another stepson was not so fortunate. He lived with a hateful situation. "My stepfather never wanted to have me around. He even referred to me as 'part of the package.' He'd go out of his way to ignore me, to have nothing to do with me. Then, when he and my mother had their own child, things got even worse."

Now, instead of merely ignoring him, the stepfather added insult to injury by lavishing attention on the new child. "Whenever they were going anywhere, he and my mother would vie for who was going to hold my brother. Sometimes I wasn't allowed in the car with them. They really never took me anywhere." As the two boys grew older, the situation deteriorated. "At Christmastime, for instance, there would always be a load of things for him and almost nothing for me, except from my grandparents. Whenever my brother and I got into a fight, my stepfather gave me the worst of it, no matter who was at fault." What are this stepson's reactions today? "I have no kind thoughts about the home I grew up in. I hated it there. And if I saw my stepfather on the street today, I'd cross to the other side."

There are some things that children have found they can do when the mate of a parent causes them more grief than they can tolerate. If the natural parent, because of conflicting loyalties, fear, timidity, or just plain insensitivity to mistreatment of the child, doesn't step in, there are other ways to survive.

- "When my brother was fifteen and big for his age, he simply stood up to our stepfather and said, 'I don't want you to ever beat me or my sister again.' "
- "My grandparents suggested that when my stepfather started to hit me, I should run into the middle of the street and scream, and that would put a stop to it. It did."
- "I think if other kids are really upset about the way they are treated, they should talk to their school counselor or their minister or someone else they can trust."
- "I tried to stay away from home as much as possible. Fortunately, my grandparents were around, and I spent all the time I could over there."

5
A TOUCH OF THE LAW

What Legal and Financial Responsibilities Might You Have?

It's been clear for a long time that just because a person becomes a stepparent doesn't mean there is any responsibility or obligation to support the stepchildren. As Bernard Berkowitz points out in *Family Law Quarterly*, "Once the existence of a 'step' relationship has been established, this in and of itself does not create rights and obligations between the parties."* It's like admiring the work of an artist. You may want him to do your portrait, but until you speak up, you remain only an admirer. Berkowitz continues: "Today there are only two ways in which any obligation between stepparent and stepchild can be established; either by statutory mandate or by a voluntary assumption of the parental obligations whereby the stepparent has taken his spouse's children into his household and *keeps them a part thereof.*"**

The legal phrase for it is *in loco parentis,* and it means literally "in the place of the parent." In day-to-day language, you can, by your own actions, become financially and legally responsible for a child if you agree—either outright or by implication—to take care of, raise, and educate him. Once you get to that point, as a Pennsylvania Supreme Court case of more than fifty years ago pointed out, "[the] rights and liabilities arising out of that relationship are . . . exactly the same as between parent and child.†

---

*"Legal Incidents of Today's 'Step' Relationship: 'Cinderella' Revisited,' " *Family Law Quarterly* 4 (1970); 210–211.

**Ibid, pp. 209, 228.

†Young v. Hipple, 273 Pa. 439, 117 Atl. 185, 188 (1922).

The crucial item is what your intentions really are. The question most courts ask is whether your attitude toward the child means that you intend to care for her and treat her as a member of your family. If you have taken over the raising of the child and you and your mate are paying the bills too, then you have a legal obligation to continue doing so unless the child already has a parent willingly paying support. If this happens, then, while you may have welcomed the child into your family and even have thought of him as a family member, you really aren't *in loco parentis*—at least not from a legal obligation standpoint.

Sometimes it doesn't even depend on financial support, though that's the clearest way of deciding whether or not you are responsible. Even if you aren't out making a living, you still could have an obligation for the child. In this case it's best to look at the other aspects of *in loco parentis:* Did you intend the child to become a part of your family? do you tell others that the child is a member of your family? are you actively raising the child? If this is your situation, then regardless of who is out working and who is at home, you probably have financial and legal responsibilities for the child.

Wilma and Walter have been married for almost eight years. Wilma's daughter by her first husband is grown, married, and living several hundred miles away, but Walter's daughter, Noreen, is not quite fifteen and has lived with her father and stepmother ever since they were married. Noreen's mother is still alive, though she hasn't seen her daughter in almost six years. Wilma was widowed when her own daughter was quite young, and to support herself she started a small shop, which has now become a successful business.

Then, last year, Walter began to have shortness of breath, dizzy spells, occasional blackouts. Arterial blockage around his heart was diagnosed, and a risky bypass operation was proposed. For Walter a major concern was Noreen. Suppose he didn't make it through the operation?

Walter's unease gave Wilma pause. Just what were her responsibilities to Noreen? She knew they had a good, easy relationship, warm, even loving at times. She was the major female influence in the girl's life. Noreen called her "mom" and would talk to her about many things she wouldn't dare broach to her father.

Wilma wondered what it all added up to. "After all these years, Noreen's just become a part of my life," she recalled, "and I love her just as much as if she were my natural child."

Though Wilma wasn't aware of the strict legalities of her situation, what had happened was that she had become *in loco parentis* with Noreen. And it suited her just fine.

Once Walter had come through his operation successfully, she sat him down, and they talked about what needed to be done for his daughter. "I told him that we should do some planning for Noreen, that neither of us had given much thought to that up to now. I told him I wanted my daughter to have the antiques I had inherited, and he should begin to think of getting things for his daughter. In fact, I urged him to begin accumulating something for her now."

Walter responded quickly, even though material things didn't matter much to him. "He went out and bought her lovely bedroom furniture—I said every child should have their own bedroom furniture; they can take it with them no matter where they go—and then he bought her a grandfather clock. Now he's redoing his office, and I've suggested he get her a desk while he orders his new office furniture, so gradually he's putting things together for Noreen."

At the same time, Wilma had to think about what she would do if Walter had another attack and didn't survive. "If something were to happen to Walter," she said, "I'd want Noreen to remain in this home, in the environment she is most comfortable with, and anything that has a personal meaning for her I'd see that she got."

As for herself? "I'd like to have enough to see our debts paid and to continue raising Noreen. I can take care of myself, I can make a living and provide the basics for Noreen, but I also want to have some insurance for her if anything should happen to me."

There are certain special areas where, once you can show some aspects of *in loco parentis*, a child could become your responsibility. Workmen's compensation insurance is one example. When a stepparent is injured during the course of his job, most states' laws allow stepchildren as well as children to recover for loss of services and support. All that's required is to show that the child had "some" dependency on the adult.

Another example is life insurance. Generally, the courts are quite liberal in interpreting insurance policies, as well as the laws, so that when words like *family* or *dependents* appear, stepchildren are implied and included. The test is whether the child could expect to have an advantage or a benefit if the adult remained alive. "In applying this standard to a 'step' relationship, more than the mere relation of stepparent and stepchild is needed to create any presumption of a 'benefit.' "* The child has to show some type of dependency on the adult, some expectation of getting aid or benefits when they are needed. "Again, the question of dependency is a matter of the stepparent's intent."**

Then, in the area of public assistance, or welfare, the big issue is whether the income of the adult should be taken into account when benefits for the child are being considered. Unfortunately, there is no common opinion, with some states requiring an *in loco parentis* relationship and other states not. It would be best to check the requirements in your particular state, since they can range from the mere fact that the stepparent knew of the stepchild's existence at the time of the remarriage to the stipulation that the stepchild be actively residing in the stepparent's household. In any case, if you, the stepparent, are unclear as to whether or not you are obligated to support a stepchild who wishes to apply for welfare assistance, you can find out easily enough through your state employment security office or department of welfare.

You can also take yourself out of the *in loco parentis* relationship and thus cut back your legal and financial obligations. Everything is based on your intention, so once you intend to treat the child as something other than a member of your family—as a boarder, perhaps, or a visitor—and you act accordingly, you have removed yourself from the parental role. At best you become a caretaker, sharing a home with someone else's child but not sharing much of yourself.

On the other hand, where you are willing to become or remain *in loco parentis,* the weight of the responsibilities should be more than matched by the knowledge that the child looks to you for guidance and training. Though Bernard Berkowitz speaks of it in terms of stepfather and natural mother, it could just as easily be the other way around. "A stepchild has an important interest in the role of his stepfather for the maintenance of his physical well-being, his social and intellectual development, emotional stability, and his place within the 'family' entity for economic, heritable and other legal incidents. The mother's interest (as she is usually the natural parent) is in

---

*National Life & Accident Insurance Co. v. Parker, 67 Ga. App. 1, 19 S.E. 2nd. 409, 422 (1942).

**"Legal Incidents of Today's 'Step' Relationship," pp. 209, 220.

the well-being of her child and in creating a strong family unit in order to maximize the success of her marriage."*

Planning Your Estate

Suppose you've just inherited from an aunt an illustrated first edition of the works of the Romantic poets, and you know from family conversation that it could be very valuable. You are also a stepparent, and you have your own child from a prior marriage. It would be nice, you tell yourself, if that child could get the first edition when you die so that it can stay in the family.

One certain way would be to give the child the complete works *before* you die, but then you never really intended to relinquish them during your lifetime, because you want to be able to enjoy them while you live. Another method would be to rely on your mate to see that your child gets the books when you die, knowing that your mate "would do the right thing." But suppose your mate has no intention of "doing the right thing," or suppose your mate dies before you? Either way, your child could be cut out of this inheritance, unless you have a will that makes clear what your intentions are.

The very nature of the stepfamily, with its intricate weaving of parents, stepparents, and half parents, half brothers and half sisters, stepbrothers and stepsisters, speaks forcefully for the need for some device that will clarify, distinguish, and delineate exactly what a person wants to do with any property he or she might own. The most appropriate device is a will.

Yet we have found that surprisingly few stepparents have given it much thought. "There's a real reluctance on my part," says William Riggs, a Portland, Oregon, attorney who is both a father and a stepfather, "and probably this is true for everyone. As a professional and a disinterested third party, advising a couple contemplating marriage and having stepchildren, I'd say do something about it soon, but when you're in that situation yourself, there's almost a mental

*Ibid., pp. 209, 228.

block, because I have all these different concepts of how I would want to handle things, and I keep wondering about what the fair way would be."

From a stepfather who is *not* a lawyer: "Wills are something my wife has nagged me about ever since we got married, and I've never even spent a minute thinking about it. My insurance will go to my wife, and I'm sure that there wouldn't be any problem between her and my natural children. I think she would give them their share. But up to now, I've never thought about this problem. Maybe I will, someday."

From a stepmother; "My husband chose to include my two girls equally in his will about four years after we were married. Prior to that time nothing had been done. I never really thought much about it, because I was very naive as far as finances go."

One stepparent who did think about a will was a Florida lady, and that may have been because of her business experience. When she married Fred, her son was college age, and Fred's son was only six. "When you get married again," she said, "you have 'yours,' 'mine,' and 'ours.' As soon as I married Fred, I gave up a trust fund that was left to me by my first husband's family (it actually went to my son when I remarried). Now I had to think about that and about my business, which I've had for twenty-one years, and it's harder to keep up with your business when you've got a new husband and a small child around. So we had to work out the 'yours,' 'mine,' and ours' thing. I've got a lot of antiques from my family, so we furnished our home mostly with my furniture and china, and I said to Fred, 'These antiques have got to go to my son. I don't want to appear selfish, but they all come through his grandparents and include things I've accumulated, and I just think they should go to him.' So we each made our will."

Even when you write a will, you must be careful. Suppose you have become so attached to your stepchildren that you regard them like your own, and you make no conscious effort to distinguish between them and your natural children. Then in your will you set out the things you want for your "children," will the stepchildren be covered?

They might not be. A New York case almost 150 years ago set the general rule, and many states in this country still follow along:

The legal meaning of the terms "issue," "children," or "grandchildren" and of every word of that kind, when used in a will to describe persons who are to take the property, applies only to those who are of the blood of the testator, or of the person named as the parent, and such terms . . . do not include those who may have acquired the name or character of "children" by marriage unless there was a clear intention to the contrary effect expressed in the will.*

It has nothing to do with an *in loco parentis* relationship but derives rather from the words used in the will. The courts must then decide whether the person who wrote the will *intended* his or her stepchildren to be included when only the word *children* appears. Only where an ambiguity over the meaning of the words crops up can you look elsewhere beyond the language of the will and prove that there was an *in loco parentis* relationship sufficient to have the stepchildren included.

But note that the problem can be completely avoided if you, the stepparent, state specifically in your will that your stepchild or stepchildren will get so much and your natural child or children will get so much. Distinguish between the two, for purposes of your will, and you can rest with the knowledge that the law will do what you want it to do.

The classic way to handle the differing interests of stepparents and stepchildren is through the use of a trust—giving a life interest in your assets to your mate and then directing that the ownership of the assets pass to your natural children and/or stepchildren when your mate dies. "A trust," according to Michael Beausang, a recognized tax and estate planning authority and an attorney, "is a vehicle for doing two things after your death. One is to give someone the ability to own your assets for the period of the underage of your children; the second is to make an outside party (the trustee) responsible in a fiduciary capacity for picking up the interest of the trust and making sure it gets to the right party at the right time. With stepfamilies the major concern seems to be that the surviving spouse won't take care of his or her stepchildren, so this is where some kind of trust or prop-

*Barnes v. Greenzebach, 1 Edw. Ch. 41, 28 ALR 3rd. 1307, 1311 (New York, 1831).

erty control comes in. Basically it's more appropriate when the children are under twenty-one, because beyond that age they are pretty well capable of taking care of themselves."

Beausang points out that by making a life interest in your property for your mate, you allow for the continued use and enjoyment of those items (including money, of course) that both of you had when you were alive. Then, too, there are some tax advantages. "Setting up a life estate for my second spouse is not the kind of interest that is taxable at her death. So you can bypass any death taxes in her estate altogether." He does advise, however, that when this arrangement is worked out, you put in a provision that the trustee can invade principal "for support and maintenance" of your surviving spouse so that maximum beneficial use of the trust assets can be made. It doesn't change the tax consequences.

Let's go back to the family heirloom situation again. Can a trust be worked out here too? "If you give that set of first editions to your four-year-old son, he won't have the vaguest notion for years of what rare books are, so the only person who could safeguard his interests would be your mate as executor, who by means of the trust would be under a fiduciary responsibility to see that your son got it when he reaches majority."

Suppose you never get around to writing a will and you have children or stepchildren you really care about, can this cause problems? The answer is an unqualified "yes." When a person dies without a will, he or she is considered to die "intestate," and then the law of the state where the person resided will set forth who gets what. This will be those who are legal relatives, spouse, children, even aunts, uncles, sisters, brothers, parents—*but not stepchildren.*

Danny is a case in point. He was raised from babyhood by his stepfather and mother, and after his mother died, by his stepfather alone. Yet he had never been adopted. When Danny was eighteen, his stepfather married again and, within a year and a half, was killed in an accident. His stepfather left no will.

Danny recalled, "My stepfather told me that he had put money away for me for college, two days before he died. Afterward I found out there was just a few hundred dollars, and I was really surprised and shocked. He had life insurance, though, and a large settlement from the accident, which went to his new wife. I've seen nothing. But it's a touchy subject. I don't want to go up to my new stepmother and say, 'Where's my share of the money?' She tells me that she has put money aside for me, and I'm lucky, because she doesn't have to give me anything. There's also furniture in the house that belonged to my family, but I don't think she'll ever give me any of that. I think she believes it all belongs to her."

If Danny's stepfather had made a will, Danny wouldn't have problems today. Another device that would have been useful here is the antenuptial agreement. "The execution of a will and an antenuptial agreement at the time of remarriage go hand in hand," attorney Beausang says. "The main reason for the antenuptial agreement is to preclude the new spouse from claiming property rights after marriage—and by reason of the marriage—that you didn't intend." By this device you and your spouse-to-be agree that the property or a portion of the property each of you owns at the time of the marriage will not be subject to the claims of the other by reason of the fact you had married. So, in effect, the only thing that would have passed to the stepmother in Danny's situation would have been that which Danny's stepfather specifically wanted her to have. Property that he and Danny had shared, as well as money for education or whatever, would not have been subject to her acquisition.

The estate planning methods people use depend to a large extent on their philosophy about how much help they should give their children and their stepchildren. A good attorney or tax person with some estate planning background can suggest the appropriate mechanism for you, but you have to decide for yourself just who or what it is you want to protect, why, and for how long. Each of the following stepparents have done exactly that:

- "If I should die, as long as my husband doesn't remarry, our home stays intact for him and my stepdaughter. But if he remarries, then the furniture, silverware, and other things from my family will go to my daughter. As long as he lives and doesn't remarry, everything stays the way it is."
- "I have a trust fund set up for my children, funded with life insurance, that essentially will see them worry-free until they are about twenty-five years old. What I'd like to do eventually is ensure that my kids are well taken care of with life insurance in the trust, and most everything else would go to my wife."
- "We figured that *our* child should get most of what my wife and

I have in case something happened to both of us because she is still very young, and the others—my stepchildren—are old enough to take care of themselves."

Should You Adopt Your Mate's Child?

A psychiatrist says: "I think it's ideal to adopt one's stepchild if the motivations are honest."

An attorney says: "I've set up trust funds for my own two children. I don't think I'm emotionally or financially ready to make the same commitment to my stepchildren. If I adopted them, I would feel duty bound to do so."

A doctor says: "I've provided equally for her children and mine in my will, but I don't think she should adopt my children. If I died, she would be hard put to raise five children alone, so I've made other arrangements for their future."

A government employee says: "You have to recognize that stepchildren are not yours. I don't even think adoption makes a difference."

A fashion designer says: "I haven't thought through adopting my stepdaughter. For one thing, her and her father's religion is different from mine. I could see that as a problem."

A teen-ager says: "I could hardly wait to be adopted and be like other kids with a father."

The reasons for and against adoption are even more varied than some of these responses. At first blush it seems a noble thing to cement a relationship between stepparent and stepchild, to give the child your legal commitment and, often, your name. It's a big step and well worth careful consideration.

Psychiatrist Gordon Livingston considers it from the standpoint of the relationship between you and the child. He believes that in adoption this relationship is the only one that really matters. It is as unreasonable to expect that adoption will make you feel closer to the child as it is to expect that a marriage will make you love your mate more. Your relationship with the child must have been cemented *before* the adoption.

"It really is a statement of permanent commitment," Livingston says. "I think before one goes into something like that, one has to be reasonably sure that the relationship with the child will sustain direct parenting. If adopting is considered out of anything except a sense of commitment to the child, then it should be avoided."

Dr. Livingston works with many foster children, and he draws on his experience to make this comparison. "It is analogous to the foster home situation. No matter how good the foster home is, there is a lack of that formal statement, the legal paper or whatever it is that makes a child feel truly a part of or attached to someone else. It's missing here. So, from the child's point of view, adopting is ideal, but your reasons better be the right ones."

What's a wrong reason, we wonder? Trying to wipe the natural parent off the face of the earth, for one, says marriage and family counselor Joanne Frankel. "The mother who urges her new husband to adopt her child or children often does so because she wants to erase the fact she was ever married to the child's real parent. But this parent can't be denied. In cases like this, the child, later in adolescence, will probably seek out the real parent whose claim had been forfeited by adoption. The child will be saying, in effect, to the people who raised him, I resent that you denied me knowledge of my real parent."

A 1969 study at the University of Toronto School of Social Work showed that only one quarter of the men who became stepfathers by virtue of marrying divorced women adopted their children.* This is not a surprisingly low figure, considering the legal obstacles to adopting a child while the natural parent is still alive. Not many fathers or mothers are willing to give up their children easily, and the law is quite clear that in most instances, natural parents must give their consent to any adoption. There are exceptions, of course, such as the parent's abandonment, mental disability, failure to provide support, habitual drunkenness, child abuse or neglect, or ex-

---

*Benjamin Schlesinger and Eugene Stasiuk, "Children of Divorced Parents in Second Marriages," in *Children of Separation and Divorce*, ed. Irving R. Stuart and Lawrence E. Abt (New York: Grossman Publishers, 1972), p. 32.

tended imprisonment, but the burden of proving these exceptions generally rests with those who want to do the adopting.

Yet parental consent is only part of the issue. The child's wishes (unless he or she is a baby) should be considered. Dr. Benjamin Spock, a leading advocate of children's best interests, has this to say in his book *Problems of Parents*: "My own inclination, as long as there is no great urgency, would be to wait until the child could participate in the decision, at least until eight or ten, preferably sixteen or eighteen and out of the vacillations of adolescence. Meanwhile he could be given most of the sense of acceptance, with his stepfather's intention, by being told that his stepfather would like to adopt him as his own someday if the child should decide. Meanwhile he could use his name informally if he wished."*

One teen-ager who had been "informally" using her stepfather's name for years was anxious that he adopt her. Her natural father had kept up contact with her for years and raised strong objections. But the teen-ager felt closer to her stepfather, "and she felt more a part of this family than her father's family," her mother said. "But it wasn't easy to get her father's consent. When my daughter was seventeen, her father finally agreed, saying, 'I'll allow the adoption if you'll forgo all the back child support and anything in the future that I'm on the hook for.' My husband fortunately has enough money to take on all the obligations for clothes, medical bills, and college."

Not every stepfather is as fortunate. The decision to balance financial loss against emotional gain is a tough one. A New York stepfather said, "It would be nice to adopt these kids, but that social security check coming in for their care every month is pretty nice too. We don't want to lose that." And the same could be said for any inheritance the child might get or any income from trust funds or any support from the natural parent. All of these items could be wiped away if you went through with an adoption.

Some divorced men who are paying child support and also supporting their second wife's children are chary of adoption. If *this* marriage should ever break up—and almost every twice-married person considers that possibility at one time or another—he could be caught with even more child support payments. For one such unfortunate, the second divorce is not yet final, but because he fell in love

*Ibid., p. 248.

with his little stepchildren and then adopted them, he is now responsible for their support, as he is for the support of the children of his first marriage. He'll be in hock for years, he speculates, but one thing is for sure: The next time around he won't adopt—if he can afford a next time around.

In some instances we found that the decision not to adopt was used as a real reminder that the children were, in fact, stepchildren and would never be considered anything else. One girl related that when her stepfather got angry at her and her sister, he would frequently turn to their mother and say, "They're your kids, not mine." Sometimes he would add, "Thank God." Was there any legal barrier to adopting them, we wondered? "There wasn't. If he had, I think our relationship would have been different, more honest. He might have felt freer to love us or take more pride in us instead of being a constant critic."

None of the children we spoke with regretted being adopted. One girl whose adoptive father had subsequently divorced her mother wonders where her brother, sister, and she would have turned if it hadn't been for him. Her mother is utterly unstable and ruthlessly selfish, and the children all clambered to live with their adoptive father. If he had not adopted them, his responsibility for them would have been much more nebulous, and they would probably not have felt secure enough to call on him for a home.

For these children, as for most others, adoption means that the stepparent cared enough to go the very limit. They like the security of sharing a name, of being somebody among their peers, especially if their natural parent is dead. Another girl recalled, "All three of us were glad to be adopted. That was all I wanted. I started junior high, and my name was changed that first year. I insisted that everyone call me by my new name, and I corrected them when they forgot. It was very important to me. I was so anxious to have my new name."

The emotional side of adoption is most important. Every professional we talked to stressed that it must be something you want for the good of the child, because you and the child have a close tie that is separate from the relationship you have with the child's parent. "Examine the motivation," we were reminded again and again.

Linda and Larry and their big family have worked out well. Larry has three adopted children, together they have one natural child of the marriage and two foster children. The home is a well-disciplined but loving oasis. Larry explained. "The reason I adopted my wife's children was to make more of a family unit. We asked the kids how they felt about it, and they were enthusiastic from the beginning. The practical aspects were certainly a consideration in my decision to adopt, however. If the children had been receiving child support or social security, I would have explained the financial facts to them and let them know I loved them just as much and would adopt if we could do so without depriving them of the things they needed. They knew I wanted them, though. Yet we didn't jump into it. We let it take its natural course over a period of months and made sure their real father was willing to continue staying out of the picture.

"When our own child came along, she just filled in with the others. Nobody thinks in terms of not being sisters and brothers. When the oldest girl and boy told their younger sister I wasn't their real father, some time back, she said, 'Who are you kidding?'

"I can't think of myself in any way except as the father of all of them."

Custody and Visitation Problems in a Living-Together Arrangement

The essence of the living-together arrangement is the lack of legal strictures. It can be a casual, open-ended sort of thing, with neither party committed to any long-term resolve, or it can be a full and total commitment for a lifetime. In either event, the strength of the entire relationship rests on the personal will of the two people—and to many judges and lawyers this is where a possible threat to society lies.

For the one thing marriage can provide is stability. There are secular and religious laws and customs that govern the conduct of the marital partners and their rights and duties toward one another, toward any children, and toward society in general. But there are few such guidelines for a living-together arrangement, and so long as the two people remain unmarried, many outsiders will treat their relationship with jaundice, apprehension, even hostility.

It's best to distinguish between how the courts view a living-together situation and how an individual—the spurned spouse in particular—might look at it. Most judges are people in their fifties and older, and more often than not they are appointed because of their political views and background, not because of their sensitivity or their libertarian philosophy. The chances are they learned the moral difference between right and wrong more than a generation ago, when the sanctity of marriage was more secure than it is today and the great majority of people who lived together were free-thinkers.

It's only human that such attitudes affect the way a judge will eye a custody or visitation matter. His or her guiding principle in these cases is "the best interests of the child." And the aim will be to award custody or determine visitation with the child's interests paramount. The judge is supposed to be objective in all this, but it's fairly easy to see that if he or she was raised to believe that marriage is the strongest tie, then awarding custody to those in a living-together situation would fly in the face of that—unless the alternatives were far worse. It's fairly certain, though, that where a person vying for custody has a living-together arrangement, most judges will lean in the direction of giving custody to the ex-spouse. They may invoke behavioral professionals to testify about the damage the child's psyche could receive as partners move in and out of the household without strings, but the essence of their decision will be grounded in their biases learned many years before.

Of course, judges don't decide these cases by rote. They evaluate all the relevant factors, including the kind of home the children are currently living in, the age and sex of the children, the livelihood and life-style of the respective parents, and the children's declared preference. Often there are behavioral professionals who have interviewed both parents and children and are willing to give their views on where custody should go. But in the end, it's the judge who makes the decision, and, in the loneliness of his chambers, who knows where his biases might take him?

The spurned spouse will generally react to a living-together situation much more emotionally and negatively than will the courts. It's hurtful enough that the marriage broke up, but then for the former husband or wife to begin living with someone else is an additional wound. The objectivity of the judge is now replaced by the subjectivity of the spurned spouse, and this can make for nasty consequences, especially where the children are concerned. Somehow the idea of giving up a marriage for the uncertain state of living together can be more offensive than remarriage, as if the person were trading in an ocean liner for a rowboat.

One man described the lengths to which his living-together partner's ex-husband threatened to go. "Theo was married to an attorney, and he really raised hell. First, he announced he was going to sue me for alienation of affection, and then he swore to her that he'd never give her a divorce. In her own mind she figured the only way she could really get out of that marriage was to give him custody of the three kids, so that's what she did."

It's been more than two years since the divorce was final, but that hasn't lessened the bitterness and hostility. "It's all still there, and it probably always will be there. There's no question he'd still like to get some revenge for losing his wife, even though he's remarried now and has a much more interesting life."

There really isn't much defense against someone bound to use the custody laws and his or her own children as weapons against the spouse who walked out and started living with someone else, except to hope that time will smooth things over, that the children will eventually grow up and understand, that the judge might begin to get the picture. But we'd advise you, if you are in a living-together arrangement, not to become too optimistic and to keep your custody expectations lowered.

Occasionally, the spurned spouse is able to rise above the bitterness and anger and to become more objective. Such was the case with another attorney. "When I found out that my wife had left me to go and live with another man," he said, "I sat down, and in as lawyerlike manner as possible and as quickly as possible, I tried to figure where the ground lay. I told her I would really like to take the children, that I was probably better able to care for them under the circumstances, since she was going to be in a period of great adjustment."

His wife agreed to the custody arrangement, no doubt believing that this was the price she had to pay for living with someone else. But her husband had no intention of cutting her off from the children. "Then I said that I expected her to assist me in raising the children, and to that end she could see them as much or as little as she liked, that she could keep a key to the house. I've left her with certain charge accounts that she's able to use for the children, and once a month we have lunch and talk about what's going on with them. One time I buy, the next time she buys."

How has this affected the children? Their stepmother says, "I envy the relationship they have with their mother, and there's nothing I would ever do to jeopardize it. She calls me every week, and we talk about the children. While I sense they have some resentment toward her, I can't think of anything worse than trying to bring it out and talk about it. She may not have custody of her children, but she's very close to them."

In some ways, visitation can be a more damaging tool than custody. Visitation is an ongoing arrangement that brings the parents into contact on a fairly regular basis, and this affords opportunities to vent hostilities over and over. As we saw, living with someone else can act as a red flag to a spurned spouse, and often, with visitation, it's the new mate of the natural parent who gets the brunt of the attack. That's because the living-together arrangement is something the ex-spouse can point to as a "moral" issue, as a "degenerate" influence on the children.

- "For the first six months when we were living together and John picked up his daughter for visitation, he was told not to bring her anywhere near me. He stuck to his wife's wishes, and this made me feel very low."
- "I guess Tony's ex-wife doesn't care for the way we are living. She's made some comments to his sister and refuses to let him bring his daughter here for a visit."
- "It wasn't until we told her we planned to get married that she allowed Bill's boys to spend the night with us."

The living-together arrangement still remains a threat to society's establishment. Visitation for a natural parent who is living with a new mate can certainly be a problem when there is a hostile ex-spouse in the picture. Your best bet is to try to work everything out between yourselves, avoiding judges and lawyers. For once negative rulings are put on paper, change is next to impossible.

As the mate of a parent, you should know that visitation and custody can be jeopardized by a living-together arrangement. A judge joining with a moralistic, vindictive ex-spouse can make it tough to get equal time with the kids.

6
LIVING WITH OTHER PEOPLE'S CHILDREN

Temporary Care—Children in Crisis

In a narrow sense, when we talk about a temporary living arrangement, we're deviating from the pure stepfamily framework, because the word *family* implies a continuing relationship, and a temporary situation doesn't qualify. But many of the principles that should operate in stepfamilies—such as the need to set behavior limits and to come to terms with your expectations—also work when your grandchildren or your nieces and nephews or your friend or neighbor's child moves in for a month or a summer or even a school year.

These are other people's children too, and even though they may only be with you for a limited period, your way of life will change—sometimes pleasurably, sometimes not.

Understanding why the child is in your house in the first place and the effect he will have on everyone else living there is the key. It could be a death, serious accident, divorce, severe trouble in school, or perhaps a family member's lingering, debilitating illness.

What can you expect to happen?

Psychologist Gary Margolis cautions, "Inevitably the child is going to throw the temporary family itself into something of a crisis. It's not going to be business as usual. Schedules are going to change, patterns are going to be altered, yet so many don't understand this will happen. The temporary parent goes on a rescue mission, thinking, 'I'm the good guy who's going to take this poor unfortunate in.' But after a few days reality sets in."

The "poor unfortunate" is living, breathing person in a crisis. And the effect on the person's behavior is often not pleasant to be around and can be disruptive to the settled life of others. Among the effects are that—

- the child will undoubtedly be masking most, if not all of his real feelings
- the child's behavior could become infantile
- you probably will feel a heavy intrusion on your privacy

More than likely, the crisis will throw the child into panic and fear, though the older she is, the better will she be able to handle her feelings. But in any case, her behavior will be a direct response to the frightening events. If she comes to live in your home, you should be aware not only of her probable underlying emotions but of her attempts to cope with them.

For example, when a child suffers a parent's death, there is a panoply of reactions he will experience. "There's a tremendous grief reaction to the death of a parent," says Dr. Margolis, "a tremendous amount of sadness and anger in response to the death. What happens is that these feelings are going to be masked, so the kid coming into a temporary living situation is probably going to be demonstrating behavior and feelings that cover up the pain and anger at having lost the parent and at having to leave the primary home, the neighborhood, and the group of people he was comfortable with."

The various stages in the grief reaction are fairly predictable, though you may not experience the gamut of them if the child lives with you only temporarily. First there is denial, the refusal to acknowledge that the parent really died. According to psychologist William Dowdell, "It can be very disturbing to the adults that the child doesn't seem to comprehend what is happening."

Such was the case of a twelve-year-old boy who refused to believe that his father had died. Before his death in a car accident there had been many months of bitter squabbling inside the family. When his father didn't come home, the boy assumed his mother had thrown his father out again. Not even the coffin made a cogent impression. It took months before the boy exhausted the last bucket of tricks to deny the reality.

Pure unbridled rage is the next stage in a child's grief reaction—anger at the world, at the parents, both living and dead, because there are no answers to the frustrating questions, Why is this happening to me? Who are you to leave me? Your visiting child may very easily strike out at her environment, and you could find your windows broken or the kitchen a mess. It's possible to help this child, and Dowdell suggests, "In effect you should be doing one thing with your right hand and another with your left. You should try to support and understand the child and the reality he is facing, while at the same time maintaining order and limits within the house. Urge the child to take out his rage in more nondestructive ways—punch the pillow, hit the mattress, run around the school track."

It might also be noted that even the smallest children can have a reaction to the loss of a parent. Those who haven't reached the talking stage can still sense the hole in their lives, and behavioral professionals tell us they might react by not eating, by continual fussing, by a general nonresponsiveness. Such a pattern might well go on until someone else takes over the nurturing of the child and soothes the unhappiness.

For the older child the grief reaction doesn't stop with rage. There is a form of bargaining after the fact. "If only I had been there when it happened, I would have . . ." The child feels guilty and takes on the responsibility for the death. Dowdell continues, "This is followed by a level of depression, and a child in a home on a temporary basis can make everything pretty spooky for the adults and for the rest of the family. The adults ask themselves what they can do to make the child happier, the child becomes a weight around everyone's neck and continues to mope, and this begins to drag the entire family down."

The way to cope with this is gently to prod the child to participate in family functions, though at a reduced level. The child should not be allowed to maintain herself as an island, but by the same token, it isn't necessary that she be pushed into a heavy role within the family. One example would be the family picnic—the child should go, but needn't rollick and roughhouse if she doesn't want to. Encouraging a child to be there without the need to become intimately involved is a good approach.

The last stage of the grief reaction is the acceptance of the death, the realization that life does go on. The cycle is now complete, and if the child living with you has come to this point, you should be able to treat her as you would another guest. The important thing to remember with the entire grief reaction—and, to a slightly lesser extent, with any other crisis situaiton—is, as psychologist Gary Margolis says, "to acknowledge that the kid living with you temporarily is feeling something, that you aren't going to discount the reality . . . even though you may not fully understand it or agree with it."

Any child coming into a temporary home from a crisis situation will be full of stress, and one of the important things you will have to deal with is the scope of unacceptable behavior you can tolerate. The tendency, of course, is to let your emotions take over and permit sympathy to override your better reason.

Carol and Jim were inclined to feel this way when their grand-daughter, Julie, came to stay with them, but they soon realized that this wouldn't be fair to the child or to themselves. Their son had died after a lengthy hospital siege, and his wife—their daughter-in-law—was suffering from such a grave depression that she was clearly unable to care for Julie.

"What bothered me most," Carol recalled, "were Julie's habits and life-style. She hated to get up in the morning and would never get ready for school without being prodded. She was a television addict and would spend every waking moment in front of the set. She was used to eating at odd hours, usually peanut butter sandwiches."

For the first week or so, Carol let Julie have the run of the house, until she realized that all she and Jim were running was a hotel. That's when she started to draw some limits, though not without a bit of pain. For when Carol scolded Julie for rolling on her satin sofa, the girl gave her grandmother a kick in the shins and then cried and cried because of homesickness. Wisely, Carol did not chastise her but concentrated on getting her absorbed in other activities. "I drew her away from the television set by getting her into the Girl Scouts and into a youth group at our church. Then we rented a piano, and we arranged for her to have lessons, but at the same time, Jim and I sat down with her and worked out regular hours for going to bed and getting up."

Within a few weeks Julie had settled into a routine that brought a relative calm to the household. The fact that there was no way of knowing when her mother's depression would lift was not the disturbing thing it might have been if Julie's grandparents had not offered her structure and affection to replace the great uncertainty and fear that came from the crisis of her father's death and her mother's disability.

Sometimes the behavior of the temporary live-in child can test the resolve of even the most patient adult. Such was the situation with Leo, a fourteen-year-old whose father had moved to another state in order to start up a new business. Leo's father had arranged with friends to house Leo until the end of the school year, when he would send for him. Leo's mother and father had been divorced several years before, and Leo and his mother had not seen each other for more than two years. Within a month after moving into his temporary home, Leo began to get into trouble. The psychologist who is treating him now told us, "Leo began stealing from the people he was living with, but in the course of his stealing, he always made sure to leave a trail so he would eventually be caught."

Why? "To get to somebody, to force the issue, to say, 'Hey! I'm living with these people, I don't want to be here, I'm going to have something happen, I'm going to have society act for me, I'm going to force the issue.' And that's exactly what happened."

What bothered Leo was that he really didn't believe his father's story about sending for him at the end of the school year, so, according to the psychologist, he hoped to create a large enough incident that the father would have to come and get him. In the meantime, the people with whom he was living had to decide what to do with him. They finally agreed to let him stay on, and they handled the entire matter quite well. "When they caught him, they were consistent on limits," the psychologist said. "They didn't say, 'Oh, you poor kid, your father is a hundred miles away, you need more love.' They confronted him straight away and said, 'Look, this stuff is missing, we know you did it, and we want you to pay it back.' " Since the family lived on a farm, they gave Leo a regular allotment of chores, and they set an hourly wage for his work. For each hour he worked, this would be a credit against what he owed them. It took him more than four months, but eventually he paid back every cent.

With very young children the behavior may be different in content but no less undesirable. "A very young child, a six-year-old, for example," says psychologist William Dowdell, "might regress, act younger, suddenly wet or soil the bed or their clothes at school. The child will unconsciously act as if he or she were younger, when the world was nicer, when there was no stress or crisis. They might also go back to thumb sucking, to carrying a blanket around . . . to any act that's too childish for the particular age. It's a very effective and necessary defense mechanism against the terror and the panic of the present."

On the other hand, some children—and they run from very young to much older—might jump forward "and assume a parental role, the 'little prince,' who always says the right things and does the right things," adds Dowdell. "But this isn't a real kid, he's operating with a tremendous self-defense mechanism." And psychologist Gary Margolis would agree. "Frequently, these are the kids who wind up two or three years hence coming to my office with a serious depression."

A child arriving on your doorstep in the midst of crisis can be a pitiful thing, evoking every ounce of sympathy, kindness, and protective instinct. But the very emotions you feel could be the downfall in your ultimate relationship with the child. It's one thing to provide a safe haven for the child and quite another to think of yourself as the child's savior. A Maryland woman described her feelings about the thirteen-year-old girl who had literally arrived on their doorstep a bit more than a year before. "We thought we could 'save' her from harsh grandparents and an irresponsible mother and father. But living with her has been difficult at best, and it has caused some severe rifts in our marriage. The biggest thing I've had to face up to is that while I don't want to cut the ties with her completely, I definitely want to go back to a friend-friend relationship and get away from the mothering thing." But of course, if this woman hadn't set out to assume a rescuer's role in the first place, she wouldn't have expected any more than she got.

Expectations still remain a prime source of difficulty in temporary living arrangements, and often the adult who seeks to "save" the child is victimized by it. "With a lot of people, the rush to help in an emergency situation can bring some unwanted consequences," says William Dowdell. "The neighbor who offers to take Johnny in for a month because there has been a tragic auto accident is often giving release to an emotional reaction, but as the honeymoon effect disappears, people frequently find they have extended themselves more than they ever wanted to, and they get resentful."

Vera experienced these resentments after sixteen-year-old Shari, her daughter's friend, came to stay for the balance of the school year. Shari had been living with her own mother, but things had grown intolerable because her stepfather (her mother's fourth husband) was abusive and her mother alcoholic. At first, Vera's expectation ran the gamut of the rescue emotions. Shari needed to be treated like a daughter (unrealistic), Shari should respond as if she had sixteen years of careful upbringing (impossible), Shari should enjoy sharing every moment with her new family (ridiculous), Shari should behave just like Vera's daughter (improbable).

Vera recalled, "Shari had been living her own life before she came into our home, and within bounds she wanted to continue to do so. It took me awhile to realize this. She was used to doing her own laundry and became uncomfortable when I wanted to take over the job from her. She liked eating standing up, slurping yogurt or salad, while I like to set a linen and candle table. One day I bought her a blazer and slacks, but she never wore them. All she wanted was a see-through blouse and crotch-tight jeans."

What finally helped Vera was a talk she had with a psychologist friend. "She told me I was trying to smother Shari, that she was a born survivor who had been through horrendous times and wasn't about to become the instantly mannered daughter I envisioned. 'Turn her loose,' she advised, 'give her a bed and the room she needs, be there if she wants to talk to you, but don't try to be her mother.'"

The resentment that Vera felt because Shari didn't respond in the way she expected soon gave way to a more realistic attitude. "Instead of having someone who was not about to be grateful to us for 'saving' her from her own terrible family situation, I found a young girl who was pleased to be with us for a hassle-free time, who felt herself a guest in our home and expected to be treated that way, and who would share certain family privileges and family responsibilities. It made everything much easier all the way around."

One important way in which to avoid a "savior" approach is to prepare the other members of the family carefully so that they don't overreact to the temporary live-in child. Just as you attempt to understand the stress the child is going through, so should they. But it's advised that you not overdramatize the situation nor so oversensitize the other members of the family that the newcomer feels stigmatized. This could result in your own children thinking, "Here comes this weird person into our family." Then too, you could build up unreasonable expectations—"We expect this kid to be bitter or angry"—and the newcomer will have a hard time filtering through the expectations that have been created. Better to limit your preparations to just a couple of sentences about the child, gently making other family members aware of the situation.

One fairly common complaint from adults who take in a temporary live-in child—and this is true whether the child is a relative or not—is the lack of privacy. If this child were a permanent resident, for instance, you likely would come to terms with the lack of privacy, and if it remained a bothersome thing you could thrash it out with your mate. But there really isn't any comfortable way to handle your complaints about the temporary live-in child, because the family dynamics in the midst of a crisis are much different.

Behavioral professionals tell us that the best guard against an invasion of your privacy is a thorough knowledge of yourself and the limits of your tolerance. Can your household amalgamate a stress-filled thirteen-year-old with equanimity? Will an emotionally distraught seven-year-old bring added tension and disruption? Are you already concerned about how much your natural children have limited your privacy? You can be sure that no matter how many people there are in your current household, the addition of a child in crisis—even for a temporary period—is going to cut back on your privacy. Are you willing to pay that price?

Obviously you might feel an overwhelming sense of responsibility for such a child, especially if you are a relative. There may be no alternative than for the child to stay with you. In these instances you had best resign yourself to the temporary loss of privacy and hope that what you lose will be more than made up by the help you can give. The real trouble appears when the adult isn't prepared to face this and then becomes resentful when there are no sanctuaries left.

A Philadelphia woman described her growing anger at the ten-year-old girl whom they took in "temporarily" as a favor to divorcing friends. The girl, Sandra, is still with them and does not want to move back with either parent. The "temporary" mother has had a new baby in the meantime. "We've really lost our privacy, and it's taken its toll now. It wasn't so bad last year, but this year with the baby, there's just no time or place for my husband and me to talk. She doesn't seem to understand our needs even when we spell them out."

Another woman told us about her feelings when her two nieces and one nephew came to spend the summer. Their father had been in an auto accident, paralyzed from the neck down and on the hospital's critical list. The children arrived twenty-four hours later, joining a household that already held four children and little space. "I remember feeling desperate once in a while because I had no quiet place to go. Everything was in a turmoil, I was constantly frustrated."

Her husband, however, organized the children's activities so that they would be kept busy and out of doors. "Each age group had functions," he recalled. "My oldest son and his cousin—because they were older—slept in a hut away from the main house, but during the day it was a marching army of labor. The kids built our sidewalk and helped to lay slate tiles. I was building a barn out of old lumber, so I had all of them pulling nails, two hundred from a board, and they lugged sand in the wheelbarrow. My eleven-year-old daughter and her ten-year-old cousin made all the sandwiches for lunch and did the laundry. I was glad to have all the help, and those three kids come back and see us now and talk very positively about that summer. They even enjoyed the work, because they were doing it together."

Though the child in crisis may come to you with problems and you may feel the weight of his burdens, it need not remain this way. The child coming out of a traumatic situation may desperately need the kind of relief you can provide. You might, just as eagerly, sense a special pleasure in being there when the child needed you. The giving of temporary care in a stress-filled situation is fraught with difficulties and problems, but there can be a happy ending. As Dr. Margolis points out, "It is encouraging and relieving for a child to move away from deeply distressing events and to join a new family. There can be real joy and good feeling in this—not only for the child but for the adult as well."

Temporary Care—a Home Away from Home

"The first time I thought about sharing our home—even for a temporary time—I was a little fearful of how everything would work out. It was pretty exciting for me to learn I could adjust to taking someone else's child into our life." So said a woman who has brought five teen-aged students into her house over the past ten years.

There is no doubt that the moment your door is open for your young guest, be he relative or friend, your life will change. Just as importantly, so will the life of the temporary family member. But the crucial thing is the reason why the temporary relationship has come about, and this should dictate the kind of interaction between you. The child visiting grandparents for a holiday, for example, is in quite a different situation than a young person coming for part or all of a school year. Joyful anticipation goes with the former, a foster-home situation might better describe the latter.

Where there is no crisis, you have a better opportunity not only to decide *if* you want another person in your home but also how you'll handle it. How will she meld into the family? How do the other members feel about bringing him in? How will you define limits and expectations? How far can the rules be bent? How would you settle that very important issue of finances? How will you involve her in your activities or in the neighborhood?

Discussion within the family before you've said, "Come in," is crucial. Even small children should know where they stand in relationship to the newcomer. Within every household there is already an established system of behavior and rules which will either accept or reject the newcomer. Even though you long to say, "We'd love to have you, come on in," this reaction may be only a polite surface response and not representative of the feelings among others in the family.

Psychologist William Dowdell feels that family discussion is the important first step to a successful visit. "First," he says, "I would work it out with my mate. Then I'd prepare the kids. Probably the thing the kids are most interested in is territory. They'll want to know where this newcomer is going to sleep, 'Am I going to have to move in with my sister or brother? Is he going to get my bedroom?' You have to establish your own child's security and communicate that this disruption isn't a severe thing and that it can be fun." Most important, he concludes, "the children must know that their security is not going to be traded for someone else's."

Territory was an important issue in Janet's family, and she made sure that none of her children felt they were being displaced. "Before we took in Sonia for the school year, we knew we'd have an extra room for most of the time she'd be here. Our son was in boarding school, and we could borrow his room while he was away. But I explained to Sonia that when he came home for vacations, she'd have to bunk in the den , because this was his permanent room. There was never any trouble about this, but I'm sure if I had taken over his room completely, he would have felt hurt and jealous."

Are you going to give the newcomer more time and attention than you give your own? Do your kids understand why you may have to do this, so they can better handle the jealous pangs when they sprout? Janet and her family discussed sharing their home for months before the event. The kids were as anxious as she to bring a new face to their table. But Janet was careful not to be so generous with her time and affection that her own children had to suffer. "If you find you are going out of your way to treat this person better than your own, you can expect difficulty," she said. "I realized it when I would help Sonia with her schoolwork to a much greater extent than I had done with my own kids. My oldest daughter, especially, had her nose out of joint for weeks until we were able to talk it out."

Melding into the family takes imagination and effort. "It was my sixteen-year-old daughter who suggested Ronald come live with us for a while," recalls widower Michael. His daughter had taken over running the household since her mother's death. Ronald was a fifteen-year-old whose father didn't want him; he needed a place to stay, and it seemed logical he could move in with Michael and his three teen-agers. "He casually appeared one day after we had agreed we liked him and had the room to take him in. Ours was an easy household with few rules except to show up to eat the dinner our cook made. Rooms got cleaned up about every two weeks. But before Ronald moved in, we all painted his room the colors he wanted and fixed it up as a welcome to him. We had an old piano, and he took to it right away, never having touched a piano before. Fortunately, none of us mind strumming, and there was nobody to tell him to shut up. Everyone more or less left everyone else alone, and we let Ronald play for hours. I guess because we were easygoing, he didn't feel like an outsider. We included him in everything we did, fixing up our old boat, going out on picnics, and so forth. Since all the kids got along well anyway and love each other very much, he was just included. I think that's important. If there's friendliness among the family, then your guest seems to respond to that and blend in."

There was no set agreement about how long Ronald would stay. "It was pretty much the understanding that he'd stay until one or the other of us got tired of the arrangement. But at the end of four months I decided to remarry and move. So that ended it. Very nicely, too."

The question of finances is one that many hosts refuse to face realistically, yet one that behavioral professionals feel is extremely important. Many families think that discussion of money, when it comes to caring for children, is crass. The prevalent feeling is that you can't equate hospitality with money. This is nonsense, and unless you're really well off or the child's parent or relatives are completely destitute, you owe it to yourself and your charge to bite the financial bullet.

Psychologist Gary Margolis voices the professional viewpoint about finances when you take on the care of other people's children. "It is very important to talk about this before the youngster comes into the house; otherwise, conflict is going to develop around the money question. The rescue fantasy of saving the child soon becomes shockingly unreal as you see how many dollars' worth of food is being consumed and how much is being spent on hot water. Since you, as a temporary parent, would feel embarrassed about going back to the person responsible for sending the child, the one who will bear the brunt of discomfort over the money will be the incoming child. It's wise to establish a very good contract."

Involving the child up to the limits of his understanding is also wise, Margolis feels. The youngster should know where the money is coming from that's being used to support him and whether there are any responsibilities on the child for doing something in return for his support."

Aunt Lillian, who took her college-age nephew in for the school year, was not reluctant to take money. "I'm not afraid to discuss finances. Everyone knows I don't have much." Her nephew's mother didn't have much either, but Aunt Lillian wouldn't allow that to be an excuse for her to assume all financial responsibilities. "His mother offered ten dollars a week, and he was free to complain about the quality of the food as long as the quantity was sufficient. Of course she paid all his school expenses."

The pitifully low amounts offered to host families is amazing. But even more shocking is the discovery that many children are taken in with no help offered whatsoever. One surrogate mother, in anger at the financial situation into which she and her family have been locked, says, "Of course I wanted to take Barbara in, and still want to keep her, but do you know how much a thirteen-year-old eats? She makes my husband look like he's on a diet. And her rich grand-parents, with their Rolls-Royce, send us seventy-five dollars a month. It's just the right amount so they can deduct her on their income tax."

Developing a clear understanding of your own family's financial situation is imperative. Money is not a dirty word until the lack of it becomes a source of irritation, resentment, and destructive emotion.

There is general agreement that defining espectations and limits is necessary for peace of mind. This holds true no matter whether the temporary boarder is a granddaughter, nephew, or just a friend. Aunt Lillian, recalling the school year her eighteen-year-old nephew spent with her, says, "We got along fairly well with only a few hard-and-fast rules, which I expressed as reasons. For instance, I maintained that a three-minute shower is legal but a forty-minute browse in hot water is not (the high cost of water and sewer). I didn't make an issue about small things such as wet underwear drying on the porch railing or bathing suits dropped over the sundeck. I saved my clout for major things, such as being home by eleven thirty and no dates on school nights and no smoking upstairs. The eleven-thirty rule was because I needed my sleep, no dating on school nights because he was living with me for a serious purpose, not to squander his days. No smoking upstairs was rationalized because of the fire hazard. Of course we both recognized and discussed that most of the requirements were for my benefit, not his. Be on time for dinner—I don't want to spend the evening in the kitchen. Let me know where you are—I'm too old to handle worry."

What about rules for behavior that didn't directly concern Aunt Lillian? "I didn't think he could have two bosses, his mother and me. If she let him smoke and drink, then I would too, except for some regard for overfilled ashtrays and possible fires. If she let him take expensive trips or spend money on records, fine with me. That was not my territory."

This sharing of responsibility can have its good points. Aunt Lillian found she could get along with her nephew better than she had with her own boys, now grown and gone, because she was not solely responsible. Since good humor is one of her virtues, she avoided letting anything become too large an issue, finding, too, that the light touch achieved more than the most impressive oration.

Psychologist Dowdell believes that rules can be handled with grace as well as firmness, and he suggests that adults communicate clearly what the bedtime and mealtime rules are, getting the youngster to understand that there are differences from house to house. You should point out, "Maybe this or that wasn't expected of you at home, but this is the way we do it here." Says Dowdell, "A child should never have the power to feel that his rules will prevail in your household, although as the young person gets older, he needs less and less structure and can be given more power to decide things for himself. Yet even with an eighteen-year-old you should make it very clear that you're in charge, that you run the household this way, and that the visitor is expected to do some adjusting. Yet hopefully you will be ready to expand your tolerance to give effect to his greater maturity."

Dowdell joins other behavioral professionals in believing that all children need structure within which to operate. "I think it's verging on cruelty for a child to come to believe that he has more power than the adults, and this will only happen when the adult really gives permission for this to happen. A child needs to know for his own protection where the borderlines are."

Bending the rules becomes not only sport but a deep power struggle for many kids who are living in a temporary arrangement, especially when it's with a relative whom they think they can manipulate. Psychologist Gary Margolis would side with the host in a situation where a youngster has a choice of whether to visit or not and knows the rules but doesn't expect to be bound by them.

He says, "The person who is creating the problem is the one who is trying to bend the rules. Inevitably this will bring bad feelings. What is necessary is to lay out expectations ahead of time." If they come into conflict with a life-style the youngster has become used to, then you as the parent or the host may have to reevaluate whether the visit should proceed. Even if expectations are rigidly narrow, the youngster knows what they are. "Then he will have a fair idea of how far he can put up with them or to what extent he can ignore them without it becoming a problem."

"My house, my rules," says Maggie, a grandmother who keeps her grandchildren for two months every summer. Yet even with this pious injunction, she adapts the house as much as possible to them. "They would be miserable if we didn't plan for them, and so would we." With that in mind she and her husband write down all the activities that they can think of to make life pleasant during the temporary stay. They also find out what foods the kids currently like best and have a few special snacks on hand. The children have their own room, with their own games or toys that have been collected from neighbors willing to share. The neighborhood itself is clued in on the visit, and the grandparents make sure that some of the same-age kids are invited to a welcoming party the day after the grandchildren arrive.

"It's not easy changing the way you're used to living, having to get up and fix breakfast early when we're in the habit, since retiring, of having coffee in bed. But the grandchildren need us and keep us on our toes." Herb is nearing seventy, demanding and touchy. "I don't think it hurts for them to know they can't get away with stuff with me that they can with their father. I've lived longer and make sure they come up to my standards. When they're here, they're expected to be polite, no running wild like they do in their father's house. I've seen them make faces when they don't think I'm looking, but I made faces at my own grandfather, and they do as they're told, even if they don't like it."

In spite of the fact that he sounds like a complete disciplinarian, Herb does become their friend. He has taught them to fish, row a boat, bait a trap, mount butterflies, clean crabs, oil a bike, mend an aquarium, raise mice, label seashells.

"Do we give up entertaining when they're here? Not on your life," Maggie said. "We love having people in, and the grandchildren are right in the middle. The youngest likes to dress up in her long dress and pass trays. My older grandson meets people at the door and takes coats or sweaters and helps serve and wash up. They talk with all the guests and show off like crazy, but older people don't mind that. We're more tolerant than we were years ago, when we could hardly wait to get the kids out of the way. Our friends make these children feel important and really welcome."

But what about "my house, my rules"? Most host families feel that it's necessary, but within reason. They don't invite breakage by leaving out delicate and valuable pieces that small children will handle no matter how many times they're warned. Most grandparents feel it's all right and sometimes necessary for them to spank. Unlike stepparents, they don't feel they have to prove anything. By virtue of their status as grandparents, their privileges and expectations are more realistic and better defined.

"And it's quite easy to exert pressure on your grandchildren when they're staying with you at your sufferance," says another grandmother. "I would not hesitate to limit a visit to just a week or two if a child refused to follow our rules. In the case of a visiting niece, I flat out told her she could not come back next summer because she had lied and refused to help around the house."

Of course, that is a luxury many grandparents can't or don't wish to have. If extenuating circumstances are such that it's impossible for you to turn the kids out, then there's no alternative than to work out the problems under the same roof.

Grandparents with whom we spoke suggested that some of the following techniques might help:

- Keep the kids busy. Get them involved in the kind of labor their parent would be unable to pursue with them. Make a list of the skills you've acquired over the years and plan some work sessions so you can teach the kids.
- Work out a schedule that gives you time alone. Make sure they can play at someone else's house once in a while—and reciprocate, where necessary.
- Enlist outsiders to teach them skills. Use the "Y," the library, the community center, the local school. Find out about programs their parents are too busy to discover and use.
- Give them a sense of proprietorship about your home. As a relative, you are in a unique position to give them a feeling of heritage. Talk about your family.

- Talk with parents who have children about the same age in order to find out what kids are doing these days. You may want to reevaluate your rules on bedtime hours, curfew, and the kind of clothing they should wear.

As for other temporary relationships, much depends on the individual family dynamics, though certain basic considerations such as discipline, behavior, and expectations pertain right down the line. But when you live with other people's children, a successful relationship must go beyond the basics, and among the children and adults we talked with, the following positive comments were offered:

- *a fourteen-year-old girl who lived with friends of her father's for six weeks:* "I reacted by becoming withdrawn. Fortunately, my hostess did not try to 'mother' me. If she had, I would have felt insulted. I needed breathing space but was glad that she was warm and included me in the chores and discussions. As an adolescent, I think they treated me just right—like a responsible young adult."
- *a woman who has observed foreign-exchange students living with American families:* "The families that seem to have the most success are those that 'do' a lot. They ski, fish, hike. They're active and get a youngster involved in the community, like a scout troop."
- *an uncle whose nephews and nieces spent the summer with him and his family:* "It helps a lot to have good neighbors who have children of their own and who don't mind a bunch of children running over their property. It helps to get the neighbors on your side, sort of like an extended family."

Is "Togetherness" Something You Must Live With?

In the past few years more and more people are enjoying open relationships and marriages. What about stepparenting? Is twenty-four-hour-a-day stepparenting necessary? Many parents' mates think it is,

158 / How to Live with Other People's Children

even as resentment bursts from every seam. Yet there are others who come to terms with how much time they can tolerate with children and seem much more relaxed about it.

One psychologist who is a stepfather and has also counseled numerous stepmothers, speaks for both sexes. "As someone who comes in as an outsider, a stepparent has tremendous responsibility to keep an even keel. Yet that parent is under the gun, under great pressure until the relationship has been established over time. How, then, do you, the stepparent, get time to recoup, to recharge your batteries?" This is somethng that must be worked out with your mate. There are times when you will want to be alone with one another and other times off by yourself. Only you know what you are accustomed to or comfortable with. Since most of the pressure is on you, the parent's mate, to adapt, it's almost mandatory that you make time for yourself so that you can get the family, kids, and yourself into perspective.

The adult who has never before raised a child is faced with a degree of closeness that the natural parent may not find onerous at all. Even if you had dreams of instant family togetherness and shared joy, they have probably gone out the window by now. If you've given up all your spare time to be a family person, you are sure to miss the outside stimuli that used to keep you keen and vibrant. You thought you married for love. Instead, you got child care, lost weekends, and the PTA. All this time out of your life, and they aren't even yours!

Why is there so much dissent in the ranks? Because we force ourselves to conform and do more than we can reasonably be expected to do. There are some steps to salvation, but first you must deal with the question of why you need time away from the child, why you're afraid to take time away, and how much time together you can manage without stomach upset, migraines, and domestic upheaval.

Not all children are easy children. A lot depends upon age, temperament, and how much trauma was experienced in the other marriage or through the breakup of it. You may find yourself dreading visits from the child, yet knowing full well that to suggest less frequent visits would make you appear cruel and crude. How do you truly feel? Chances are, even if you've admitted such feelings to yourself, you haven't opened up with your mate—and for good reason. It's a hurtful thing to say, "I really don't want to be around that child so much" or "The time he spends with us leaves me ragged." You think because you're an adult you can will yourself to act and feel in a certain way. But you can't hide your feelings forever, and eventually you will have to come to terms with them.

Patty, a young stepmother with two boys who are the product of her second marriage, feels wretched about the way her husband Dennis's daughter affects her. "I encourage Dennis to call and have the child over. One half of me wants to urge him to see her, and I think, 'This time it's going to be different.' Then the other half of me gets tense, and I can feel my blood pressure start to rise. I haven't talked this out with Dennis because I feel it would hurt him even more than he already is. But I don't think he enjoys her visits, because there's a strain on all of us when she is here."

Lucy, another stepmother, is also caught in the unpleasant weekend syndrome, and she feels virtually trapped by it. "I would like to be able to spend some weekends alone with my husband without children, but the custodial thing is such a bitter battle that my husband feels he can't give an inch because he might lose so much more. I know, though, it would be a lot better for us if I had at least one weekend a month away from the children." At this stage she hasn't given any serious thought to taking herself out of the picture for a weekend or an evening, even though she feels miserable most of the time the stepchildren are around. "Before the kids come for a weekend visit, I begin to get tense, as if I'm steeling myself for an unpleasant experience. Of course that's setting it up beautifully. I know to be successful I should be more flexible, but I've lived alone for a long time; I'm used to solitude and sleeping late on weekends."

Is it necessary to go on like this, permitting the assumption that your mate's children are part of the marriage bargain whenever it's convenient for their parents or for them to make it so? No, say the professionals. It does not have to be the lot of stepparents to lead lives of quiet desperation in the name of trumped-up togetherness.

Enjoying one another is great, but why do we feel we have to do it in family tandem? The very grouping that constantly brings a parent's mate into the picture may be the catalyst that causes negative behavior. Think a moment. Who does your stepchild really want to see, you or his parent? Who really wants to see the child, you or his parent? What are you doing crowding the picture on visitation weekend when things might be better without you? "I never thought of getting out of the house," said Patty. "I don't know if Dennis could handle his daughter and the boys, yet when I was alone for a week with the three of them, it was much better." At some level Dennis has communicated to Patty that he would find it hard to deal with the kids alone. So, feeling guilty for even *resenting* the fact that she must hang around, she sacrifices her own piece of mind 100 percent of the visitation time. Of course there are alternatives. She could take her sons to visit relatives or friends or to the zoo—anywhere for part of the time her stepdaughter visits with dad. Or he could take all three. Or he could take his daughter somewhere alone. Household discord does not have to become the main event every time his daughter visits. And Patty shouldn't have to pop extra blood pressure pills.

The same is true for Lucy. She could go elsewhere for a day or two. It isn't as if she's leaving her husband. She's only leaving her husband *free* to spend some constructive time with his sons.

Psychologist Dana Lehman-Olson says, "If the purpose and intent of visitation is to be with your kids, then you must set up the conditions where your attentions can best be with your kids." She suggests visiting alone with the children, giving some concrete thought to the kind of activities just the parent and children can share. This is not to say that the parent's mate should or must be shut out of the picture. You too can find things you might like to do alone with one or more of the children. "The principle here is to set up conditions or an environment where you can give your attention to the child."

Visitation is a grand opportunity for a parent. This is the time when the child can build memories of what a great person her parent is. It isn't necessary for you as a parent to constantly try to create a home environment similar to the old days. Go hiking, go camping, or make a picnic lunch at home for you and your child alone. Go to the store, clean the garage, put up storm windows, get a garden started. A parent is not destined by fiat to shrink behind the newspaper and listen to bellowing between two sets of children. There *is* a choice after you decide how much family closeness is good and how much is unhealthy.

On the visitation level, the imagined or imposed necessity to feel and act as a loving family unit can be more deadly to the custodial stepparent than anyone else. Since few men today are housefathers, the burden of "togetherness" usually falls on the woman. As we mentioned before, those who are especially vulnerable are usually women who have not had children of their own and are trying to assume a full-time mother role. Scout troops may love you, and the school cafeteria may depend on you, but what is going on inside of you? If the sense of family unity and total motherhood carry their own reward, fine. If they don't, then it's wise to look for alternatives before resentment, anger, and guilt eat you up.

Stepmothering doesn't have to be given up entirely; stepfathers who go off to a job don't feel conflicted in this way. Unfortunately, many people—even your mate, perhaps—may see any expression of your true feelings about this as a rejection of a responsibility you once willingly accepted. If you see it in the same way—that is, if you are full of guilt feelings—then there could be trouble. As one psychologist put it, "If a stepmother tries to build a life separate and apart from her stepchildren, it becomes almost like a predivorce arrangement. Although a person may find this the most personally acceptable living arrangement, I predict that somewhere down the road there will be problems." This prophecy has been borne out by the reported experiences of many women, for in many cases the choice of a career over a total involvement with parenting did not happen until irreparable damage had first been done by the effort to force togetherness.

However, psychologist Frank Strange says, "I've advised some people that working outside the home is by far the better alternative to staying around and suffering a deteriorating relationship with persons that they had no hand in bringing into this world."

Perhaps the question of liking or disliking your mate's children is not the issue at all. Having been suddenly engulfed in a relationship that brings along with it already formed children, you may come to the realization that you are not the total hausfrau you thought you were. "When a woman hasn't come to terms with how much of a housewife she really wants to be," says Dr. Strange, "she will become frustrated with that. Then on top of it all comes the question of dealing with the stepchildren, which she can probably handle better in little doses." This would perhaps be true even if they were her natural children, but now they are thrust instantaneously at her. "In either case," continues Strange, "I would give the same advice—that she can simply function better if she can pick the time to be with the children. Then she would feel less resentment for the obligation someone laid on her."

Professionals and stepparents we talked to agreed that stepfamilies have an especial need for time for the husband and wife to be alone together. If this time isn't set aside or given proper consideration, everyone, including the children, begin to get on edge. One stepfather observed, "My wife and I personally make it a point to spend time together, and when we're not getting enough time together, we tell each other about it. If you can't do this, pretty soon you notice the little barbs, and I notice I don't feel very good about being around her, that I'd just as soon be by myself. When that happens, I know it's time to do something about getting away together."

We've read articles by stepparents who've lived through four, five, or six on a honeymoon. It makes cute copy. That's about all.

Getting Mealtime Hassles Off the Table

Too many adults face mealtimes with other people's children as they would a horror hour. That special time that, according to all the soupy television shows, is supposed to sparkle with scintillating wit, spiritual regeneration, and yummy food is a big bust. Why?

Children often use mealtime as a subtle and not so subtle way to take aggressions out against their parent's mate. Consider how few are the ways a child has to fight with someone who is mentally and physically his superior. But one way that's wide open for his use is criticism of an adult's cooking. This kind of treatment can drive a person to an earlier and earlier cocktail hour. It helped to run one stepmother's first marriage onto the rocks, and the second batch of stepkids are going after her in the same way—at the table. She said, "The biggest issue in both marriages has been around food. I grew up in a Jewish home where it was understood you'd eat the food on your plate. While I realize it's a hang-up, there's still nothing that bothers me more than to see food wasted. I know I cook differently from the mothers of both sets of stepchildren. They made bland food, and I like mine highly flavored or foods from my cultural background. Frequently I hear words like 'Yuck' or 'I don't like that' or 'What is it?

It looks awful.' I get angry because I worked hard to prepare it. I don't like people reacting that way to food, and I feel very strongly that children are going to experience different foods in different people's homes. It's just a part of socialization that they should eat what's put in front of them. A child has to learn to deal with things he doesn't like."

Another stepmother came under what psychologists refer to as "passive-aggressive behavior" by her stepchildren at mealtimes. One child sat quietly, making no comment, but deliberately moved her food around on her plate all through dinner. Scarcely a forkful would find its way to her mouth. Her brother sat through dinner, drank his milk, and said he would get sick if he had to eat "that stuff." Promptly after dinner he would make himself a peanut butter and jelly sandwich. "They made me feel guilty," she recalled. "I wondered what I could make that would be palatable for them, but even when I got them involved in helping me cook, they'd undermine me at the table. They were visiting stepchildren spending a couple of weekends a month or a few weeks in the summer, and I thought, 'It isn't fair that I should turn myself inside out to try to cook stuff that only they like.' My husband still gets angry with me and tells me that the boy has always been a feeding problem, and anything that he could get down was great, no matter what it was or where it was. I'd look at the chicken breast congealing on his plate and seethe inside. He would have mashed it up where it wasn't fit for anything but the garbage. Then the girl would toy with her food, and I can't stand to see a kid play with food. When it was finally cold and sparks started coming out of my eyes and a few choice words from my mouth, her father would pick up her fork and feed her. She's too old to be fed, but she just opens her mouth. My husband's comment is, 'Don't let's worry as long as she's eating.' "

Adults who are faced with behavior similar to this do have other options besides letting the children spoil dinner, waste food, and scramble what should be pleasant dinnertime conversation. Children who are so inwardly angry or troubled shouldn't be part of your meal. That is not to say they shouldn't be at the table. Let them get their eating done before or after you eat, since the food itself is their weapon.

Forget the chicken breasts, beef Stroganoff, lamb roast. Find out what food they eat at home and make sure you keep some on hand.

If it's canned spaghetti and glutinous meatballs, so be it. Some children seem to subsist on peanut butter and jelly, and more than one has grown to adulthood with no other supplement than french fries and vitamin drops. Why are you knocking yourself out to try to enrich these children's eating experience? They are letting you know most vehemently that they will throw it back in your face, one way or another. Their habits are already formed, so any changes you might bring about will come slowly and gradually. You don't have to make a big thing out of it when you decide to strike for dinnertime freedom. Just calmly fix a bit of food they might eat—peanut butter for the boy if that's what he prefers—tell them that tonight they might like to have a tray in the kitchen or living room, tell them they can join you at the table to talk if they'd like and have dessert with you if that suits.

You can always measure out their size of dessert commensurate with the amount of food they ate, but never, never make dessert a prize for "finishing up." Fat adults know all too well that food as a prize is a big contributor to future obesity.

Most important, professionals all advocate that you shouldn't do battle with your mate's children over your cooking. It could become, more and more, a potent weapon of manipulation. If you sidestep, then someday you may hear them bragging about your culinary ability. They'll come around to it in time if the resentments can be laid to rest.

Children's blood sugar is low at dinnertime. Sometimes you come to the table expecting interesting conversation and are served up only whines and tantrums. This is because children are apt to come to the table cranky or ravenously hungry. Furthermore, since they might have been tearing around outside until the last minute, their hand movements may be shaky or spasmodic, so it's a time for spilling milk, splashing gravy, or dropping spoonfuls of peas. This can be modified somewhat by following certain eating patterns our grandparents took as a matter of course: A small glass of juice, milk, cheese, some celery or carrot sticks should be offered to the hungry little ones as you're fixing dinner or getting ready to put it on the table. There's nothing sacred about eating every bit of the meal at the table. Consider these pretable foods to be part of the dinner. For the late-arriving, active child try serving a cup of soup before the meat and potatoes. Maybe everyone would benefit from that. Even if she's not a soup eater, she'll be hungry enough to eat beef or chicken boullion and noodles. This will calm her down, and you may find less milk spilled. Whatever method you figure out to help the kids through a hassle-free mealtime, it's better going into their stomach than coming out of your mouth.

Some stepfathers have a tendency to make dinnertime into lecture-time. Some men who are living with other people's children can become quite authoritarian. Mealtimes, when the children are right there, visible and vocal, can turn out to be open season on manners, grades, and behavior. One stepfather, who still couldn't understand why his stepchildren didn't like dinnertime, related, "I used to have a method of trying to teach the kids manners, and I tried to make a joke of it. I had a stick that I'd keep by the dinner table. It was long, like a pointer. I told them, 'Now, if you don't do things right, if you start grabbing and taking advantage, I'm going to tell you once. If you do it again, I'm going to rap you on the knuckles.' Actually I was trying to teach them something. I figured if you do something physical, they'll remember it better." They sure did. They're grown now and avoid him like the plague.

But even if an authoritarian like this is not part of your household, you may find yourself bringing up subjects that invite lecturing. The kids get that "here we go again" look on their face or else react belligerently. A lecture is hard to take, even on a full stomach, and scolding (which is the way children see it) dries up digestive juices. Wait until after mealtime before you start on the lecture circuit.

The limits of unacceptable mealtime behavior may not have been talked out ahead of time. Some mothers don't mind if their kids come to the table with half the back lot on their hands and faces. Some fathers see nothing wrong with bare feet and a T-shirt. Some fathers don't mind children talking with their mouth full, some mothers don't mind children chewing with their mouth open. To some stepfathers and stepmothers, habits like these are revolting beyond measure. Again and again you tell the kids to wash themselves, to put on shoes, to get a shirt. Your mate can't see the problem. But *you* know that what's going on is past the limit of your tolerance. You'd better clear the air as rationally and as firmly as you can. Psychologist Dwight Mowry says that it is vital to talk out the things that offend you and the attitudes and behavior that you find acceptable. Letting things like this ride until crisis time at the table is destructive. "Ideally you should speak up before you get married," he says. Yet that's possible for too few people. They can't anticipate that attitudes can be so diametrically opposed, but it's at the table that cultural, religious, and intellectual differences can be most manifest. "Spelling out expectations and clearly defining them is a most difficult thing. I know it takes time, and I know it's hard work, but you should ask, 'Where do the kids fit in? how are we going to spend positive time with them? how are we going to discipline them? how do we get time together alone?' " If eating together is not positive time together, then step back and ask yourself if it's necessary to continue this way. Disciplining at the table, for instance, should be short and to the point. If it goes beyond that, it can be mutually destructive. If older children can't understand what you expect of them, if you aren't getting support from their natural parent, then either your expectations haven't gotten across or there is a manipulation going on between the child and the parent. If dinnertime with the kids has become an abomination, then put an end to it.

Reviewing the days' events may cause trouble. "I guess I always felt that mealtimes were the times to bring up things that happened during the day, what went on in school, who the kids played with, and so forth. But lately I've been getting a lot of static, because the things of the day don't seem to be all that pleasant." This observation from a stepfather is borne out by many others. Events at school lead into a discussion of schoolwork, which spins off into talk or scolding about grades, the child becomes defensive or angry at being cornered at the table, and dinnertime has degenerated into a sparring match.

As a rational adult, you know pretty well if the discussion you're having is going to become hot. If your mate starts to get into areas that could erupt into deep emotional disagreements, then suggest talking about it later. Mealtime, unfortunately, is a time when we are often on edge. We need a little refueling before we regain our equilibrium.

That doesn't mean that topics of the day can't be talked about. Kids love stories, and you can lead off by telling them something you observed. Are the snow geese flying south? where do they go? One of the kids might even get out a reference book in order to look up more about these subjects at the table. This is the kind of positive exchange that makes mealtime worthwhile. It focuses on no one in particular, it does not involve criticism, it does not call up negative evaluation. Planning vacations or trips can work the same way. Even if the trips are those that "we'll do someday," they excite interest beyond the food on the picky eater's plate or the fidgeter's table thumping.

It seems clear to us that adults who have never before raised children before find mealtime particularly difficult. Some are still hanging in there, suffering through the six o'clock fray. Others are making positive moves to change their own behavior—and backing off from mealtime confrontations. Says a stepfather who's feeling his way into the second year, "I followed my wife's advice and finally shut up at the dinner table. Now I'm listening, and I think it's a lot easier. She was right, the dinner table is not the time nor the place to discuss difficult subjects or make negative comments."

Suppose You Want to Have Your Own Child?

"We were in Oregon," the young man recalled. "My stepfather was working in the lumber business, and we were sharing a duplex with another couple who had no children. One night at supper I casually said to my mother that it would be fun to have a little brother to play with. The next day my mother and stepfather said I'd have a new brother, and they were right—nine months later. I always felt the decision was made because of my comment."

Most stepchildren welcome the arrival of a brother or sister. In fact, none that we talked to even used the term *half brother* or *half sister*. The degree of loving kinship varied, however, with how much equality of treatment was given by the parents. Some wistfully remarked that their stepparents were nicer or more generous or less disciplinarian with the new child. Others were glad to see new brothers and sisters having an easier time of it than they did. Some expressed deep and loyal affection.

Further, a recent study has shown that when a remarried couple has a child together, the children from the former marriages are more likely to have harmonious relations.* The reasons are elusive, but psychologist Dana Lehman-Olsen suggests that, "Sometimes when there is a new baby in the house, it takes some of the anxiety off the couple. . . . It becomes something that involves all the family and minimizes the self-consciousness in the other relationships. The child becomes the one common bond that everyone is related to."

Self-consciousness in stepfamilies is a regular phenomenon. There seems to be all that underlying stress, everyone busy watching how they are going to get along: Is this person getting more than his share? is that person allowed to do something the others aren't allowed to do? A baby, then, can give everyone a point to focus on, or in Dr. Lehman-Olson's words, it becomes a "facilitating type of thing."

Though having a new baby can make the family more cohesive and enjoyable, that is not the reason generally offered for having a child, just a welcome by-product of it. The foremost reason, particularly for stepmothers who have never had children, is, simply, to have one of their own. "My stepdaughter kept asking me why I wanted to have a baby," said a Tennessee stepmother. "Wasn't it enough that I had her? I told her, 'But I don't have you. You aren't really mine. You have a mother, and I'm very close to you, but I want the same experience your mother had. I want a child that is a part of me."

Since this stepchild was the younger child, she probably felt threatened that she would be replaced. Psychiatrist Gordon Livingston recognizes this as a major concern of stepchildren, especially younger ones. "They're afraid the new baby is going to be loved more, or cared for more, or given more. This is especially true if the stepparent is noncustodial. The child can then feel extra threatened about being shut out by the parent he only visits."

Learning about a pregnancy seems to bother children much more than when the baby actually arrives. One little girl cried unconsolably when her father and stepmother told her they were going to have a baby. It really angered the stepmother that the child should take on like this when she herself was so happy about it. Her father

*Lucille Duberman, "Stepkin Relationships," *Journal of Marriage and the Family* 35 (May 1973): 290.

fumed at her, asking, "What's the matter with you? Don't you care about having a sister or brother?" She hadn't considered it in terms like that. Through her tears she said, "The baby will get to live with you, and I can't."

Once the baby arrived, those dreadful fears and dismay eased up. The father helped too, by spending extra time with his first daughter, going to school events, watching her perform, taking her shopping. "She still wants the assurance that she's my baby, although that started to ease as soon as her sister was born. She's trying to like the baby, and I think as time goes on, she will."

Apparently children aged four to twelve have the most difficult time adjusting. This is a vulnerable period, and it's full of insecurities. It's also the time when most tensions develop within the step relationship. Child psychologist Jean Chastain cautions, "Before a new baby comes into the family, hopefully, many of the hidden problems can be resolved so that there is a free and open relationship between the stepparent and stepchild. Then they will be able to say, 'It's a neat family we have, and we're going to have a brother or sister."

If you want to have a child and your mate doesn't, there can be serious trouble ahead, unless the motives are laid out and understood. One stepmother felt absolutely cheated that she had to help raise her husband's two, when he adamantly refused to have any more. His reasoning was substantial enough for him—he was financially strapped. But he couldn't communicate this adequately to his wife, and she considered herself a poor second to his first wife. "I figured, how could he have two children with someone he says he never loved and refuse to have any with me, whom he professes to adore." The marriage finally ended, and she married another man with kids, but one who is willing to have more children.

There is the stepmother who, having gone through a couple of years tied to home and kids, says "No more.' Back to work she goes, anxious to be done with the whole at-home-mother bit. Her husband is baffled and thinks "One of our own would make a difference." Not so for many who find, after being cooped up with kids, that they just don't care for child rearing that much. Unfortunately, many stepmothers feel guilt ridden by this attitude, and some have succumbed to getting pregnant. One stepmother who escaped back to her career said, "I think I'd advise any woman who is marrying someone with children or who thinks that having her own child is going to be super different, to look deeply within herself to see if she really wants children. This is terribly important. I should have done it before I quit my job to raise stepchildren. But at least I didn't compound the problem by having one of my own."

Having a baby to patch up a shaky stepfamily relationship is a big "don't" on everyone's lips. You may end up with two groups of children, searching for a new spouse. Dr. Edward Rydman, former executive director of the American Association of Marriage and Family Counselors, says in an article in *Harper's Bazaar:* "If a new couple want to have a child of their own they should do it out of love. In no way will a baby cement an ailing marriage."* He says this with specific reference to the stepfamily.

Another reason for not having a new baby is a fearful one, yet mentioned too frequently to be ignored. Some stepparents are actually afraid for the safety of a baby. Many parents have blind spots about their children and don't recognize extreme jealousy or psychotic behavior. One stepmother who has avoided having or even adopting a child in spite of her husband's urgings recalls the horror she felt when her stepdaughter, in a fit of jealous temper, secretly and cold-bloodedly squeezed the life out of her pet hamster. "I was truly afraid to bring a baby into this house. Now that's she's almost full-grown, I would chance it, but I feel I'm too old to start again."

A stepmother who did have a baby while also rearing a borderline-psychotic stepson said, "I never left him in the house alone with the baby, not even when the child got older. I always had a baby-sitter or took our baby with us. It was awfully tense, not knowing if his deep sullenness or rages would be turned on the child." Fearing that a baby can be a potential victim of an emotionally unstable stepchild is undoubtedly more fear than fact, but the shadow of doubt that creeps into a stepparent's mind can act as a powerful deterrent to expanding the family.

But if things are going well in your family and you want to have your own child, then you should try to get your stepchild involved in the new-baby experience. It's really quite easy to make her still feel wanted, still special. It takes a little imagination, patience, and empathy.

---

*"Advice to Second Wives," April 1973, p. 105.

One stepmother told how she brought an older boy and girl into the picture. "He was sixteen and basically gentle and loving. I told him the little fellow would look upon him as a hero someday, and it probably would fall to him to teach him to throw a ball, ski, and fish. I urged him to handle the baby as soon as he was born. His fourteen-year-old sister got into the act too, and it really liberated me from constant child care. They took him everywhere, played with him like a doll, got him talking before he was a year. Now he's considered gifted, and I think all their attentions helped. He was constantly stimulated by these two teen-agers, and since I didn't hold onto him as if he were my possession, they assume credit for all his good points."

Another stepmother who took on two very young stepsons, then had a baby of her own, said she prepared the boys by learning everything she could about their babyhood. "I got all their baby pictures from their mother and father, put them into books, found out when they did this and when they did that. Then I would regale them with stories of their early days. They would feel the baby in my stomach, and I'd tell them that's the way they felt in their mother's stomach. I never showed any preferences toward my natural child over them. I simply couldn't, because I had made an effort to make these boys part of me. When the little girl was born, they helped with small things and helped pick a name. Sometimes the younger boy will look at her and say, 'I wish I could say some of the funny things she says that make you laugh,' and I hug him and tell him that when he was three, he did too. At each step of her development, I recount to the boys the things I knew that they did. I say, 'I wasn't there, but dad was, and he told me. We talk about the things you did all the time.'"

Different Races in the House

Most of us who live with other people's children would agree that anything that highlights our differences presents an opportunity for conflict. The mere fact that an adult and child—or two or more children—come from different families and live under the same roof creates tension enough. But when the people involved have widely separate cultural origins or do not share the same skin color, the potential for conflict is geometrically increased. Child psychologist Jean Chastain has counseled many interracial couples and their children. She says, "I would tell the parents that this is going to be a very difficult thing for the child, and while the parents have their love to keep them warm, the child isn't a part of that. Any child who is a stepchild already feels he has a lot of problems, so when you add the interracial aspect, it brings many, extra difficulties."

Sometimes the adjustment is hard enough even without the mixed racial atmosphere. One twelve-year-old boy had an extremely frustrating experience trying to convince his mother that it was just impossible for him to regard his Japanese stepfather like his natural father. "No matter how determined the mother was," related the professional who had counseled the boy, "he could not escape the reality that he didn't look like his stepfather, had a dissimilar cultural heritage, and had a real father living somewhere." The mother was trying to erase the memory of that bad first marriage not only in herself but in her son as well. That was difficult enough for the boy to deal with, "but the sheer improbability that his Oriental stepfather could be anything but a stepfather caused him deep emotional anxiety."

Another form of reaction to a mistaken first marriage can end in rejection of the child by the custodial parent because the child's racial characteristics are such a clear reminder of it. This is what happened in Donna's second marriage, when she discovered her new husband's attitude toward his son. The boy's mother had been Mexican, and Donna's husband was fair-skinned and blond. The boy, by the time he was ten years old, had come to resemble his mother quite closely, with his swarthy skin, jet black hair, and broad face. After the divorce the father rejected him almost immediately, and Donna realized that it was because of the racial characteristics, which reminded him of the boy's mother. So she went out of her way to be nice, even though the boy's father never gave his son more than grudging acknowledgment. "The boy was always very sweet to me," she recalled, "and one time he said to me, 'Donna, it's better to have you around.' My approach was never to assume I could be his mother, but I did look after him, and, in time, even his father became a bit more civil."

A major source of difficulty for the interracial child is identification—just who is there that the child will be able to identify
with? If the child is rejected by the parents of the first marriage, there
may be no one else to turn to but a parent's mate. Lee was a young
Korean girl who had been found on the streets of Seoul. A Christian
orphanage took her in, and within a few months she had been
adopted by a California couple. She was less than three at this time,
but most of her body was covered by scabs and sores. After she
arrived in the United States, it took more than a year before her skin
cleared up, but then two years later the couple that adopted her split
up, and the woman simply did not want her. So the husband
reluctantly took her, and they both moved in with Renee. "Lee was
diagnosed as developmentally and socially retarded," Renee said,
"though she was not mentally retarded. But she was quite hostile,
and this made it extremely difficult for me to get close to her. There
were times when I thought the child was going to be the cause of a
split between me and her father." But that has not come to pass,
mainly because Lee found in Renee a figure to identify with. Renee is
Mediterranean, a sun seeker, and always has a good tan. "Lee is
really quite alienated, you know, but the one thing she likes about
me is that she thinks of me as 'brown.' Her father is very fair, and my
skin color is more like hers. This is also what she likes best about
school. She's surrounded by 'brown' children—Chinese to me—but
brown to her."

Different manners and habits can be sources of conflict if you let
them be. When your mate's child is in your home, then, generally
speaking, your rules should prevail, but you must also temper this
with an understanding that since you weren't a part of the time when
the child learned this behavior, your expectations should be lowered
a bit. Dina is a Japanese-American now married to a Japanese-
American. She has two stepchildren, both boys, one of whom lives
with her and her husband. The other one lives with his mother, who
happens to be Caucasian. This stepchild visits from time to time, and
at first Dina was appalled at the general lack of respect and the ill
manners this boy showed. "Japanese families have their own style of
raising children," she recalled, "and since my husband and I were
both raised this way, we tend to expect it from other children. One
of the most important things is that you have your manners in full
force no matter where you are, it's a measure of respect that you

show to others." But her visiting stepchild was not used to doing things this way. "There's very little 'yes, please,' 'no, ma'am,' and 'thank you.' " Her patience, however, has finally paid off—she didn't rail at him because he was different, she didn't make cutting remarks or otherwise reject him. She began to show him bit by bit what she wanted, and "he knows now what's expected of him, and he pretty well stays within it."

There are several major problem areas for the interracial step-family that kept cropping up again and again in our discussions with stepparents and professionals. These difficulties are not peculiar to the interracial situation, but what might be easily dealt with in a non-interracial setting becomes a fiercer problem when the added pressures of mixed races are included.

Arrival of a New Baby

Unlike the situation in which all members of a family are of the same race and can thus relate to a new baby as a common focus, in the interracial stepfamily, the new arrival can be a cause of great upheaval to the stepchild. Child psychologist Jean Chastain explains: "Where a stepchild is interracial and the new family is of the same race, the stepchild is likely to be odd man out because his color will be different. Often it happens that the parent might look upon the first marriage as a dreadful mistake and go further in the other direction with the new baby and the family . . . at the expense of the interracial child, who is a living reminder of that first marriage."

Forcing a Parent-Child Relationship on a Racially Different Child

As we mentioned before, it merely takes a difference in color or racial characteristics to make even more difficult the presentation of oneself as a new parent—at least in the beginning of the relationship. But, according to psychologist Margaret Doren, we are seeing more and more of it, especially in the wake of our Vietnam experience and the untold number of orphans that were left. She suggests staying away from referring to such children as "son" or "daughter" and from insisting that you be called "mom" and "dad." She adds, "It's much better if you say, 'We're sharing our house with you, we love you very much, we welcome you, but call me Amy.' "

Discrimination from Stepgrandparents

It's different enough for some older people when their child marries interracially, but when they acquire stepgrandchildren of a different race, it becomes especially hard to handle. Most older people haven't been prepared from their early years to share their home and family with people of other races, and it makes them uncomfortable, even fearful, to be thrust into it in their later years. One young stepmother who is white married a black man with three children from a prior marriage. Her father—a conservative midwesterner—had been uneasy when they lived together but simply couldn't handle any contact with her mate's children. "He doesn't recognize them, he's a cold, immature man, and he just ignores them. My husband has had so much experience with this sort of thing that it doesn't really upset him. 'That's his problem,' he says. Actually my father seems to block out my husband's color, and they are civil to one another, until he sees the children. Then he retreats into his shell."

The stepgrandmother, however, is not so standoffish with her stepgrandchildren. She is quite fond of her son-in-law and is able to translate her feelings to his children as well. "My mother is a warm person," says the stepmother, "and she accepts her stepgrandchildren—but only when I am with them too. I can't conceive of her doing anything alone with them."

Most professionals feel that you should deal with this situation in two steps. First, you make sure to insulate the child from experiencing any more discrimination than is necessary, and this could mean reducing contacts with the in-laws, and second, you clafiry for the child that the discrimination is a particular family member's problem. "It's not you, as a person," you point out, "it's their particular bias."

Moving to a New Neighborhood

For many stepfamilies, moving to a new neighborhood can be beneficial, especially if the move takes place soon after a new stepparent enters the family. It's like giving everyone a new start, and the stepparent is not so pushed to blend in with the old scene. But it could work the other way with the interracial stepfamily. Moving may destroy the security and acceptance that the child has worked so hard to build up, especially if the move is from a racially mixed to a nonamalgamated community. "Very often," explains Jean Chastain, "the child of a mixed marriage has particular color characteristics, and these have served to give him an identity in school and with his friends." It's almost as if he has become accepted on the basis of his color or race. He has learned to cope with his environment, and moving to a new neighborhood means he must start all over again. It's doubly difficult "because in addition to the interracial thing, he has to adjust to a whole new world."

There are times, though, when moving to a new neighborhood will be of benefit to an interracial stepfamily, and especially to the stepchild. It's when the old neighborhood seethes with discrimination and trouble, when *any* move anywhere has to lessen the problems. "There's no question that such families should seek out compatible neighborhoods," says psychiatrist Gordon Livingston. "You want to be in a place where the child has a multitude of role models to choose from, such as a city or a socially planned community."

There is no magic formula for dealing with all the difficulties that spring from an interracial marriage and living with interracial stepchildren. Awareness of what might occur and preparation for handling these eventualities are probably the best approaches. "I would say to parents," advises Jean Chastain, "that they should understand they are creating a very difficult situation for their child when they start a family with obviously different racial characteristics, and it doesn't do any good to sugarcoat the situation. The parents need to know the difficulties, and they need to know that they have to take the responsibility for helping the child in any way they can."

What Should You Do About Erotic Behavior?

In many stepfamilies the time comes when easy familiarity acquires erotic overtones, when sexual attraction has to be dealt with. It can come from several directions:

- between stepbrothers and stepsisters
- from stepson toward stepmother
- from stepdaughter toward stepfather
- from stepparent toward stepchild

Unlike families where parents and children are naturally related, there is only a weakened incest taboo engrafted onto the stepfamily. The incest laws don't forbid sexual relations between nonrelated members of a stepfamily, though there are other legal prohibitions, depending on age, as well as moral disapproval from society as a whole. In the interest of maintaining family harmony—be the family blood related or not—sexual encounters between two generations within a family or between members of a family not related by marriage are considered disruptive.

Yet the taboo is frequently violated in stepfamilies. "A great number of erotic incidents never get reported," says Vera Bangsberg, a member of the Oakland, California, police Sex Crimes Unit. "The only time we find out is when one member of a family gets angry at another. But we know it's going on, and it's going on quite a bit."

Usually it's a stepbrother and stepsister who are involved with one another, and the most sensitive time is when they first start living together in the same household while entering their adolescence. Behavioral professionals are quite clear that when stepchildren of the opposite sex share a house at an early age and move into puberty in tandem, there usually isn't much of a problem about erotic behavior. But when a fifteen-year-old boy and a fifteen-year-old girl are thrust together under the same roof for the first time, often with bedrooms close to one another, how can any form of behavior conditioning work? Natural curiosity aided by proximity and opportunity could lead to unwanted consequences.

One woman we spoke with who has only been remarried for two years is becoming aware of the developing relationship between her twelve-year-old stepson and her fourteen-year-old daughter. "The two of them have very similar interests, and on a number of occasions he will go up and spend the night in her room. They sometimes sit up most of the night talking."

This twelve-year-old boy is much aware of his sexuality, for he has plastered the wall of his bedroom with nude cutouts from various sex magazines. Doesn't his spending the night in his stepsister's room concern his stepmother? "I don't see it as a problem now, and because of our family relationship, if it ever became a problem, I think we could talk it out."

What this stepmother may be overlooking is that the "problem" could be far along already. Allowing pubescent stepbrothers and stepsisters to share the same bedroom throughout the night is an invitation for them to satisfy their sexual curiosity.

"The first thing to recognize," says psychologist Frank Strange, "is that such things are likely to happen. If the adults could sit down and talk about these things and recognize that there might be problems before they actually happen, then you can change some rules earlier."

What rules, for instance?" "Modesty in the home, bathroom time, where the bedrooms are, and who can go in whose at what time. The parent can say to the child, 'I know you don't have anything on your mind, but it upsets *me*.' So it becomes an 'I' message rather than a 'you' message, and rather than pointing out that there's something wrong with the child, you simply say it's me that's responsible here, that because *I* was brought up in a certain way, certain things bother *me*."

There are times, however, when it's impossible to predict that something is going to happen. And when it does happen, you find that some people just don't believe it. A Minnesota stepmother discussed the time her nineteen-year-old stepson crawled into bed with her ten-year-old daughter and proceeded to molest her until he heard voices outside the room. "I wasn't told about it until afterward," she said. "But I found my daughter told the other children, and they laughed at her. I talked to my husband about it, but he wouldn't believe it happened. So I talked with the boy's mother and suggested she get him some help. Her answer was, 'I don't believe in psychiatry.' " The only recourse this woman had was to approach her own daughter. "So I watched things very closely after that and said to my daughter, 'If anything like that happens again, you come to me immediately, don't be afraid.' " Of course, the heretofore relaxed attitude in the family was now a thing of the past.

To a lesser degree the same problem can arise when the stepbrother and stepsister don't live in the same house, but one visits for a day, a weekend, or longer. "Where a person lives outside the home and visits," says psychologist Dana Lehman-Olson, "it should be treated pretty much as any boy-girl relationship." There should be rules about who can go above the first floor and when or who can go into whose room and until what hour. If the visiting stepchild should take advantage of the situation to the point where a real problem is developing, Dr. Lehman-Olson would have no hesitancy in treating the child just like any visitor who had overstepped the bounds. "You can tell the child not to come back again, and if your mate wants to see the child, he or she can do so outside the home."

Once these stepbrothers and stepsisters are at an age where sexual attraction is apparent, it's time for you to act. Treat them both as dating teen-agers subject to house rules concerning bedrooms, bathrooms, the wearing of sufficient clothing. "You just have to set up standards," says psychologist Margaret Doren. "If you are going out for the evening and your stepchildren are old enough to be their own baby-sitters, you should avoid leaving them alone at the same time. As a stepparent, you are going to have to remain on your toes."

The classical aspect of the incest taboo is not between brothers and sisters but between parent and child, yet if anything, erotic behavior can be more intensified. Perhaps it's because there's an adult around, and a wider variety of emotions are swirling about. Certainly there is more to it than just the sexual curiosity and adolescent fervor that exists among children.

"A girl will usually welcome a stepfather if he is an agreeable, fair person," states Dr. Benjamin Spock. "In adolescence, however, when a girl is apt to feel rivalrous with her mother in any case, as well as slightly romantic toward attractive males of all ages, she may get under her mother's skin by playing up to a stepfather or making a great show of how well she understands him and takes care of him."*

She might run through the house dressed in bra and panties, she might play with his hair, sit on his lap, even hug him or lean against him frequently, or contrive to be alone with him much too often. The professionals tell us that this can be usual behavior, and stepparents should not be unduly concerned so long as there is no overwhelming desire to encourage the behavior or to respond in kind.

A Wisconsin mother explained the way it worked in her family. "My daughter was twelve when we were married, and she just

*Problems of Parents, pp. 242–243.

thought her stepfather was the most wonderful thing in the world. She really had almost a sexual feeling for him. She was just beginning to feel her own sexual urges, and while she liked her real father, he was not as close nor as human as her stepfather, he was a bit more standoffish. She didn't want this, she wanted someone to relate to her, and I think her stepfather did."

In time this behavior tailed off to a warm, loving father-daughter relationship, with the girl exercising her sexual urges in the direction of her male peers. The stepfather, a practicing psychiatrist, had always been careful not to rise to the erotic overtures but instead had treated them merely as the normal expressions of an adolescent.

The manner of erotic moves by stepsons toward stepmothers is a bit different than that of stepdaughters toward their stepfathers. Generally, it's a bit more aggressive and blatant. There is little subtlety in the adolescent boy anyway, and when his sexual urges are involved, he is apt to be quite direct. It might be a kiss on the lips or special presents, or any of the things that one might associate with courting. It might also be the sharing of erotic thoughts, photographs, and stories—anything that might tend to excite an answering response in the stepmother.

One Oregon woman was struck almost speechless by the extent to which her fourteen-year-old stepson went. This boy, whose mother had almost totally rejected him, had been especially close to his stepmother. Then one day the first signs of sexuality appeared. "James told me he'd had a dream about me. He said I showed him thirty intercourse positions. I thought, 'Oh God, what do I do now?' I knew I had to deflect this in some way. So I said, 'My understanding is that when you dream about a woman, that's the feminine side of you, and I'm glad I'm the one who's satisfying your curiosity about sex, but you have the wrong girl here. I don't even know twelve intercourse positions—let alone thirty!' That seemed to assure him, because he never pursued it any further."

Your response as a stepparent is what will channel any erotic behavior of your stepchild into healthy, positive directions. When there are children of the opposite sex in the home, talk it over with them *before* any event occurs, set rules, and stick by them. When you have a stepchild of an opposite sex, be prepared to deflect erotic overtures without scarring the child and recognize how your conduct can encourage such behavior.

Dealing with the Strongly Possessive Child

Possessiveness is, unhappily, characteristic of most stepfamilies and is often a source of tension. A child who loses a parent by death or divorce usually clings to the remaining custodial parent.

A child's possessiveness toward her natural parent at the expense of the parent's mate can spring from several sources:

- deep insecurity, the fear of losing either or both parents altogether
- overwhelming desire to see the natural parents reunited
- plain, unadorned jealousy directed at the stepparent
- natural adolescent identification

In any individual situation there might be more than one source of a child's possessiveness, and it's helpful for the parent's mate to recognize what's behind the child's actions.

Deep insecurity on the part of Virginia's stepson led to some rough times for Virginia herself. When the boy's mother and father divorced, his mother relinquished custody readily and happily. The child had been adopted and had never been a favorite of hers. But his adoptive father liked him and was glad to bring him into his new home with Virginia. "That," she said, "was when the trouble started. At first he felt his way and did a lot of testing, and I was prepared to deal with that. But then I definitely got vibrations that he'd be happier if I weren't around, so he could have his father to himself." Since Virginia had never had her own child, she wasn't sure if this was normal seven-year-old behavior or not. Slowly his hostility toward Virginia built up as his possessiveness toward his father increased. "He'd say cruel things like, 'My dad is six feet tall, and you're the shortest person in the world and the dumbest person and the fattest person in the world.' For a while I tried to talk to him rationally and deflect his hostility, but then I began to hold my feelings and responses inside. Over the next months I developed constant diarrhea. Finally I went to see my doctor, and he started questioning me about home. Without thinking, I blurted out, 'I hate my stepson.' He told me that the worst kind of diarrhea comes from stress.''

Virginia spoke to her husband about the things the boy had been saying, and he agreed to pay closer attention and not let them pass without comment. "The boy's way of talking to me was a child's kind of punishment, paying me back for getting attention from the only parent that cared for him. Because my husband and I are quite affectionate with each other, he must have felt totally excluded.''

If Virginia had understood the boy's possessiveness from the outset, had brought him into their circle, or relinquished time so he could have it alone with his father, or simply understood the insecurity he was feeling because of the divorce and his mother's rejection, she might have stemmed the flow of his distress earlier. By understanding his motivation she could also have removed herself emotionally from his attacks.

Perhaps the most destructive type of possessiveness exhibited is when a child works to pull the natural mother and father back together again—at the expense of the parent's mate and new relationships. This is what happened to a young Michigan stepmother who had three children of her own and married an older man with five children. Her husband had a seventeen-year-old daughter who had remained with her mother after the divorce and who had almost nothing to do with her father. "But as soon as we announced that we were going to get married," the stepmother recalled, "she came back into his life with a vengeance. Telephone calls, lunch and dinner together, movie dates, shopping, anything so she could spend time with him alone. And he fell for it because he was so grateful to get her attention or approval again. But it got to the point where it totally disrupted our privacy.''

The stepmother tried to speak to the daughter but got nowhere. "She responded with a wide-eyed innocence or general surliness. Sometimes she'd go out of her way to complain to her father that I was trying to come between them. It got to be a bad situation." So the stepmother tried talking to her new husband. "But he gave me no help. 'You're an adult,' he'd say, 'you should be able to get along with my children,' and then when the daughter and I would get into a conflict, invariably he would take the daughter's side." Within two years after their marriage she sought marriage counseling but even this couldn't help. Finally there was no alternative but to divorce.

"I never realized the strength of the daughter's possessiveness," the stepmother said, "nor that she might have been acting as a surrogate for her mother. After our divorce was final, I found out that her mother had said, 'I hadn't known he wanted to get married again, because if I had known, I'd have been happy to marry him a second time.'"

The relationship a child has with a parent is his chief means of identity, and without it he will feel cast adrift. For his own preservation a child will cling to a parent. If this child has been living alone with the parent and has come to rely on their twosome, don't expect possessiveness to diminish quickly when you become a threesome. But with time and the development of other relationships of the child's own, this possessiveness is sure to diminish.

One stepfather told us that this happened with his stepdaughter. "When I married Carol's mother, we moved a good day's drive from the area where she and her mother had lived for twelve years. Now, she had never been an outgoing girl to begin with, so she had few friends. There was no family on her mother's side to speak of, so it had been pretty much she and her mother as close as peas in a pod." Once they got established in the new home, the stepfather actively sought out sons and daughters of his friends who were Carol's age and encouraged her to have parties. "We never left her at home alone to brood, and all this effort began to pay off. She's getting less dependent on both of us, her mother particularly. Don't think it's my idea of a swinging evening taking a twelve-year-old out with you when you want to be alone with her mother, but it's been worth it. Now that we're getting a lot of time alone, we realize the kid was fun to be with."

Jealousy is another destructive form of possessiveness. In many instances jealousy will peter out after the stepfamily has been around long enough to show that no one's vital interests or feelings are going to be submerged. It's an emotion springing from fear—fear of loss and change. The parent's mate who can neutralize that fear will not have to suffer from its results. There are extreme cases of pervasive jealousy, though, that really require counseling. It's the parent's mate who usually can sense when it's pervasive and deep and who will have the hard job of convincing the parent, who may truly see no problem at all.

One stepmother related that after nine years of marriage, her stepdaughter's jealousy is as virulent as ever. But until now everyone has resisted professional help. "Just last month," she said, "my husband brought me a stunning new fake-fur coat. I couldn't contain myself, but I'm open about my feelings anyway. I danced around in it, and my husband laughed and clapped, but my stepdaughter just sat very quietly saying nothing. Finally her father asked her, 'Isn't mommy's coat beautiful?' She whispered, 'It's all right,' and she started to cry and ran to her room. She wouldn't look at me for a week after that." Has this child been deprived in some way, getting the leavings of gifts and attention? "She's constantly the center of attention, and everyone puts her first. Yet she certainly is in competition with me for everything."

Possessiveness in an adolescent can be nothing more than a fairly normal urge to identify with one or the other parent. Behavioral professionals tell us that as children move through puberty, they may have strong feelings for a parent of the opposite sex, that this is merely a way of beginning to arrange their sexual urges, and as they get a bit older, they turn from their parent as the object of their affection to someone their own age. In the meantime, however, while focusing on their parents, adolescents might be quite determined to resent a parent's mate's intrusion. This type of possessiveness generally runs its course in a short time.

What do you do if you come up against possessiveness of your mate by his or her child? The most obvious answer is to understand why it's there and not to take personal affront. From stepparents' reported experiences we gleaned the following:

- Don't try to compete with the child.
- Talk over possessiveness with your mate, make him or her aware it exists, and enlist help in working it out.
- Have patience—clarifying your role in the family takes time, and time is usually on your side.
- If the possessiveness seems pathological, be prepared to seek and strongly urge professional help.
- Try to separate the child's possessiveness from your relationship with your mate, unless it's clear that your mate has no intention of working to neutralize the possessiveness.

Living Together—
a Worthwhile Alternative?

"There's a delicate but kind of fragrant difference between being married and not being married. There's just a touch of the voluntary that lingers, that would be a pity to lose."—*John Updike to Sally Quinn.* *

"Children are much less hung up on the formality of relationships than adults are."—*psychiatrist Gordon Livingston.*

Living together without sanctification of clergy or recognition by civil authority goes on all the time, and second-time-arounders in a living-together arrangement with "his," "hers," and "our" children appear to be increasing in number and steadily growing in acceptance.

Are there problems with the children? Is it really such a big deal to live together, except in the eyes of the traditionalists? First of all, there are a lot of people living together who pretend they're married. They live together because they're afraid of the legal entanglement that marriage creates, and they want to be sure of each other before getting legally joined. Yet they say they're married, either because they feel uncomfortable around relatives and friends, are afraid of what their children might think, or are worried about community reaction.

One young woman stated, "I was scared to death to marry a man with three children, and that's why we lived together for three years. Yet everyone thought we were married, including the children. He had to pretend because of his position and I because I was a teacher. We looked very respectable and kept up the façade because we thought it was essential. There were plenty of adjustments for us, and we didn't decide to get married until they were solved. His guilt attachments to his first wife had to be worked out, his guilt about leaving the children with her kept him running back to them and spending days with them. I was not about to get involved in anything legal until this had been straightened out. During those three years I also went through a maturing process, and by the time I was twenty-five, I was less concerned with myself, more giving and self-less. We began to feel naturally confident with each other and decided the time had arrived when we could get married and make a family."

The secret of their relationship was never divulged to anyone in the family or the community, and his children finally lived with them. Many people have chosen the route of a shakedown cruise like this, yet they continue to maintain the fiction that it's an around-the-world trip. If there are some stresses arising from the deception, they seem to prefer them to the problems they'd encounter if they let the truth be known.

There is no question that different areas of our nation have varying degrees of tolerance toward the living-together arrangement. The more cosmopolitan the community, or the more intellectual and freethinking the community, the more inconsequential traditional arrangements become. Child psychologist Jean Chastain, whose practice is in Berkeley, California, noted that among children she has seen, whether or not the adults are legally married does not seem to be a very big issue. "The kids don't worry about it, and the parents don't worry about it."

What children do care about, we learned, is the security that comes from knowing that things are going to continue on an even keel, that faces are not going to change with the seasons. Children *are* troubled by that, says Chastain. "If in the testing period it doesn't work out, and along comes another new person, children get very disturbed, because there really is no father or mother image, depending upon who the parent's mate is. I've had children in therapy who think of their baby-sitter as the mother figure because he or she is the one constant person who comes back over and over."

Very few professionals, regardless of how permissively the community views pad crashing and casual splitups, give much chance to a child's stability in revolving-door households. The situation is not even arguable. And the outcome for the child who is caught up in the adults' maneuvering is predictable: Just as a welfare-receiving child becomes a welfare-receiving adult, just as an abused child becomes a child abuser, a revolving-door child becomes a revolving-door adult.

A parent's mate who has not yet decided if the relationship should become permanent can expect troubled and troubling behavior even from the best of kids. They have a sixth sense, almost like animals, for detecting vacillation and unease.

"He seemed like an engaging boy when I met him," said one lady who started sharing her small studio apartment with the boy's father. "But he wasn't an issue then. Before the divorce they lived in a typical suburban setting where every child has a mommy, a daddy, or at least a bona fide stepparent. Then I learned we had to take the boy because my lover wanted him. I still gave it no thought until I heard the child say to another, 'I have a new mommy inside.' I freaked. I thought, 'Oh, no, I'm not your mother, at least not yet.' I hadn't made a commitment of any kind to his father up to that point. But he started calling me 'mommy.' I said, 'Please don't. Call me Frankie.' I honestly don't see a time, ever, when I could let him call me 'mommy.' "

It just naturally evolved, as it does for many, that Frankie and her friend would live together. They never discussed what it meant, especially the implications of having the boy. When the boy first moved in with them, he and his live-in stepmother got along fairly well, but he soon sensed that this might be a temporary relationship, especially when she made it clear she would not become his "mommy." It's no wonder that with his growing insecurity he started to become intractable and contentious when they were together and sullen when alone with Frankie. He refused to obey her unless his father ordered him to. He made cutting and sarcastic remarks, erecting barriers between them so he would not become involved with her except in a negative way. Neither Frankie nor the boy's father could see the behavior for what it was—a terrible fear of making friends with this lady if there was a real chance he'd lose her just like he did his first mother.

Frankie wrongly blames all the problems on the size of the apartment. "If we're going to continue living together, we're going to have to move. The relationship will not survive otherwise. Yet I don't want to give up this neighborhood just to accommodate the boy. I'm really not prepared to move on his account."

What is happening here is contrary to the best interests of both the child and the adults, yet the child is hurting most of all because he doesn't know which end is up. Dr. Livingston emphasizes that "fears of replacement and fears of divided loyalty are of great concern to a child. When a relationship begins to form that looks as if it will have permanence, the child should be brought into it." He was, in her words, "part of the baggage," and as it turned out, unwanted baggage. His reactions were clearly survival techniques.

Other variables that make a living-together arrangement difficult for a child depends on the age, the ability to appreciate the situation, and what the child has been told by other people. If a child's other parent says it's okay to love and live with someone and not be married, it puts a different blush on everything. Grandparents and close relatives who get into the act can also jumble a young person's judgment. One teen-ager said that since the divorce of her parents when she was four, her older sister, who had been brainwashed by her grandmother, stayed angry at her father and live-in stepmother for ten years. The relationship turned permanent, but the girl didn't put away her anger until her late teens, when she began to get the situation and her grandmother's moralistic rancor into perspective.

The most important thing that brings stability to a child during a living-together relationship is how reasonably the parent's mate behaves and how the adults treat each other. Dr. Livingston says that there's really no formula for preparing a child for this relationship except to emphasize its importance and expected permanence. Be aware that the child may be fearful of going through another grief process of attachment and separation. If it appears permanent, then it takes on the trappings of a marriage. Psychologist Dana Lehman-Olson says, "Kids perceive living together in much the same way the adults do. How they deal with it depends on how their parent and parent's mate deal with it."

The amount of parenting the temporary mate of a parent can accomplish is also dependent on many variables, not the least of which is the adult's attitude. Some stepfathers say that while they were in the living-together arrangement, they were afraid to take full control. There was always that sense of, 'They aren't my responsibility, so I'd better watch my step.' Other stepfathers assume a role of just another adult authority figure. Still others think of themselves as no more than adults who spent a lot of time with the kids. As the living arrangement takes on more permanence, many live-in stepfathers say they felt less restraint about involving themselves with the children and have less of a feeling of walking on eggs with the children's mother.

"Living together is only slightly less unrealistic than courting," said one stepfather. "You monitor your behavior when you're living together because there is always the threat that the other person can get out from under it if she doesn't like something you do. You want to look as positive as you can. Even if in the back of our head we think in terms of permanence and marriage, we still tend to curb ourselves. With marriage comes the feeling, 'I want more control over this, and I want things to go my way.' "

One New Jersey stepmother who has been living with her lover and the two sets of children—hers and his—for six months said she found nothing difficult about it, in spite of the trepidation that she had felt at first. "Before we shared my house, I asked my kids if they had any objections, because it's their house too. But they had become good friends with John; he had already stayed over some nights and helped them with their homework. He gave them kindness they never had from their own father. If they had said no, I wouldn't have gone through with it, but they were on my side from the start. I've since asked them if anything has been said at school because John's son goes to school with them and lives with us. They answer, 'Why should there be?'

"We're all content with the way things are, and I don't think I want to get married again. To me it's not important, and I think the kids understand that their stepfather is as close as anyone could be, with or without marriage. His boy and mine share a bedroom and share work around the house. They all take this arrangement in their stride."

Taking it in their stride is what we heard that most children do. That is, unless early disruption and loss hover within sight like a bleak cloud.

How Should You Handle Moodiness, Sullenness, and Silence?

"All interpersonal relationships," says psychologist Margaret Doren, "are expressed in terms of superficialities. The little things like manners and behavior usually express the underlying emotions that people feel." A child, may continue to exhibit bad table manners, for example, not because he doesn't know any better but because he knows it will drive his parent's mate right up the wall—and this child may *want* to drive the parent's mate up the wall because the child resents the adult coming into the family. Or the child may be overly quiet and withdrawn, not because he is so caught up with his thoughts but because he is confused. He genuinely likes the adult, but he hears so much criticism from his absent natural parent that it's best to say nothing.

Often the child's attitude is controlled by how he conceives his ability to love both parent and stepparent. Most children seem to believe it's something that just can't be done. So they work up an anger against the adult, and it comes out in the kind of behavior that is upsetting to the entire family. Psychologist Hannah E. Kapit describes the emotional process the child goes through: "The child who is still very attached to the absent parent and who still hopes and wishes for his return may consider the stepparent an intruder. The child may feel that this affection for the stepparent means giving up his love for the original parent."*

On the other hand, even when the child becomes fond of the parent's mate, there can be emotional turmoil. "Liking the potential stepparent may also cause conflict and guilt. If the absent parent disapproves of the stepparent, the situation holds even more conflicts for the child and needs sensitive handling of the child by the parent and stepparent, or additional counseling."** She suggests that the most appropriate way to deal with this situation is to point out to the

*"Help for Children of Separation and Divorce," pp. 223–224.
**Ibid.

child that one can love both parent *and* stepparent, that loving one is no disloyalty to the other. Merely because parent and stepparent dislike one another should not mean that the child must take sides. In fact, an astute mate should be determined *not* to engage in a conflict with his or her counterpart natural parent and should strive mightily to avoid any indication that the child can't love both of them.

One of the more frequent evidences of a child's underlying feelings about an adult comes when there is a crisis and the child tells him or her, "You can't tell me what to do. You're not my real parent." Behavioral professionals are in general agreement that most, if not all, stepchildren feel the urge at some time to remind their stepparents about this. And it will happen even though the child and adult may have enjoyed years of harmony and a close relationship. It's the most potent weapon a child has, and the more serious the conflict, the more probable is it that the child will be tempted to use it.

Marriage and family counselor Joanne Frankel thinks this type of remark should not be taken literally. "Using words like 'You're not my real parent' is the only way a child can fight back. If this child were talking to her natural mother or father, she might say, 'I hate you.'" Frankel recognizes that in either event the child is using cruel tactics, but then, perhaps, the child feels most threatened, too. She advises, "Don't deal with *what* the child says to you, deal with the emotions that prompt the remark. Deal with the feeling that causes the child to say these things."

One stepfather, who was faced with the challenging taunt, "You're not my father," wisely held down the urge to retort in kind. From the beginning he felt his wife had been lax about discipline in the house, so he went the other way, and for a while it worked. "Until they got into high school, and then they didn't want to do what I wanted them to do," he recalled. But instead of reacting in anger, he responded by saying, "I may not be your father, but you're living in my house, and I'm taking care of you, and I'm trying to be a father to you. If you don't like that, it's up to you."

Most professionals would agree that the answer this stepfather gave is the most appropriate one and that you can't sit there and argue with the child. Fall back on the reality of the situation and say it straight out: *"Of course I'm not your real parent, but that's irrelevant; we can't change how you feel, but while you're in this house, you will do what I say."*

Even this stepfather, though he answered in the best possible way, did not follow Joanne Frankel's advice completely and look to the emotions behind the remark. He couldn't help taking at least part of what the stepchildren said literally. "It's the one method children have of getting to you, and it hurts when they say it. It takes a little something from your relationship. You never feel quite the same toward them afterward."

Psychologist Frank Strange believes that the "you're not my parent" remark probably occurs in stepfamilies as much as anything else and that it is a product of the children reacting to a power struggle. "Children, by the very nature of their growing up, are opportunistic, and they will use the power they can grasp to get along in this world." Strange thinks the parent's mate should try to uncover whether the children are exhibiting their real feelings—that they really don't give credence to someone who is not their parent—or whether they have found a soft spot and are exploiting it, or perhaps both. "But I don't think such a remark is necessarily a put-down," he concludes. "It is just one way children survive until they discover they can get more with cooperation than with competition."

Most parents and their mates have noted that when a child is in the last stages of a visitation period or is getting ready to leave his home for visitation, a quietness, a withdrawal takes place. The child often will sit off by himself, not saying much, gazing away. The withdrawal should not be taken as anger or fear but rather as dismay. The child is preparing himself for the other household, for the different people he will soon be associating with. The dismay rests in the fact that the child has gotten used to the world he has been in and must now give it up. The dismay might even be touched with irritation. One stepmother recalled that her stepdaughter would not only become sad but also a bit peevish as the time drew near for her to return to her mother. "If we asked what was wrong, she'd paste an artificial smile on her face and say, 'Oh, nothing,' and then she'd try as hard as she could to show us there *was* something wrong." A stepfather recalled that in the hours before his stepdaughter would go back to her natural father, she'd mope around the house, often closing herself off in a bedroom. "And sometimes she'd be especially testy, almost deliberately provoking an argument with her mother."

How to deal with it? Perhaps the only way is to recognize that children go through these emotions and to try to avoid putting pressure on them during the few hours before such a change. When there is some irritation, it's probably directed not only at you but at the other family as well, because in the child's mind all of you are to blame for the split household that is now giving the child such grief. Don't argue back, don't be a severe disciplinarian during these times. A little understanding will go a long way.

Now, when there is a general pattern of silence with a child who lives with you or there is regular unruliness, you have to search elsewhere for clues. One of the more useful approaches is to examine how your personality or your attitudes differ from those of the parent the child is used to living with. Are you excitable, loud, demanding, forceful? Or are you quiet, calm, soft, and yielding? If the way you are is substantially different from the way the child's natural parent is, the child's relationship with you might simply be a reaction to that difference. "A child who has had a cool mother or a reserved father," says psychologist Frankie Mae Paulson, "and gets exposed to an overzealous stepmother or stepfather is going to recoil—sometimes in absolute fear—because they may not simply understand what it is that the stepparent wants. In their fantasy they may actually see themselves overwhelmed by this." The child might grow quiet as a defense to this, or sullen and moody because it rocks her secure world. On the other hand, a child who is used to a raucous household might just not react to quiet and calmness, might ignore politeness and softness—and be labeled unruly, hard to handle.

You should do some self-analysis before you plunge into stepparenting. You should have some notion about yourself as a person. Are you warm? is your humor perceived as humor? does the child think of you as frightening? In effect, is the child's attitude a direct reflection of the manner in which he perceives you? For it is you who will set the pace for the way you will be living with someone else's children. As Frankie Mae Paulson points out, "The responsibility of trying to make a good relationship initially lies with the adult by virtue of the fact that supposedly we have more experience and we can be more objective."

And it's fair to say that if we use these skills, we'll probably have fewer moody, sullen, and silent children.

Helping the Stepchildren Feel a Part of the New Family

Edward recalls he was in third grade when his teacher asked each person in the class to draw a family tree. He wrote the name Edward, then drew a line to his mother, another line to his father and a third line to his stepmother. He drew a line from his mother to her parents, from his father to his parents, from his stepmother to hers—her mother, stepfather, father, stepmother. Eight grandparents he penciled in. The teacher asked him if he knew them all. He told her yes, then pointed to his stepmother's stepfather. "I play trains with him." He pointed to his stepmother's father. "He taught me how to fish."

Now, nine years later Edward cannot differentiate between them. He refers to all of them as grandfather and grandmother, although he sees his stepmother's family more frequently. Most children adore the idea of big families, of being kin to many people. What difference can it really make if it's only by marriage?

The children we spoke with were eager and happy to be included in their stepparents' families. Some of their best memories and good feelings came out when they talked about family reunions, picnic get-togethers, visits with their stepgrandparents. Others who feared rejection or weren't sure just where they stood in the family structure were apprehensive. A college student, Paul, recalled how he felt coming into a large family after being an only, lonely child with no real relatives. "My stepmother had a big family, and at least once a month there would be family reunions of thirty or forty people. Sometimes it would just be because of a nephew's birthday. I thought that here was the family I always wanted. But there was never a family get-together for my birthday, and I wondered where I fit in. Sometimes I'd sit back in a chair and think of what it might be like twenty years from now, if I'd bring my own family around to this group. I wondered what they thought about me. I've never asked them. Do they accept me as one of their cousins? When I've been with them for a day and they introduce me to strangers, they never say, 'This is my cousin,' as they do with the others. They always introduce me as Paul. Just Paul. They say, 'This is Paul.' "

If Paul's stepmother had been more empathetic or if she had realized how much he wanted to belong, she could have paved the way more easily. A few words here and there letting it be known that he wanted and needed a family, that he was now in fact their cousin just as much as anyone else in the family. If she had only introduced him as "your cousin Paul" to her nephews and nieces, it would have set the tone for the months and years ahead.

In addition to the desire to be included in the stepparent's family, many children feel strongly about having a place of their own within the household. If the stepchild is a visitor, it might be no more than a bed and bureau, but so long as it is inviolate and constant, this is what counts. It is especially this child who needs to know that she has a place, that this is also her home.

One stepmother who has four children living at home and three stepchildren visiting on weekends makes sure the stepchildren's bureaus and closets are stocked with extra old clothes, sweaters, sneakers, and pajamas. "If they know what clothes they have over here, they don't have to pack so much. I think it makes them feel less like visitors. Their bulletin boards have crafts and pictures they've put up over the years. When they come in, they check the chore board in the kitchen for weekend jobs that must be done. For instance, this weekend I'm going to get the eleven-year-old to do some mending. It will be the first time she's used the sewing machine, and after she's done with this job, she'll feel that the machine is as much hers as mine." This mother has worked at blending the two sets of kids, often watching for sales so that she can buy matching T-shirts or windbreakers for each of the seven children. It's a little something extra that sets them apart as a family, she believes.

When two sets of children begin to live togther, it becomes highly important that a room of one's own or space of one's own be arranged as soon as possible. Think how you feel as a guest in someone's home if you're borrowing their convertible couch, taking space from their already crowded towel rack, pushing your suitcase out of sight in a cluttered closet, or cramming your things into one shallow drawer.

A stepmother who moved herself and her two children into the home of her new husband and his two children commented, "My children have had to do a lot of adjusting. I can see my stepchildren pondering, 'Whose home is this now?' They tend to become quite

196 / How to Live with Other People's Children

possessive about the material things in the house. None of this comes out directly, but you can pick it up when they're arguing or you can interpret it from some of the things they say. Intellectually they are trying to be fair. Our furniture is stored in the garage, but my own children don't care whose furniture is part of the house. All they want is their own room. The oldest daughter keeps pestering me about getting the addition put on the house so she can have a room of her own and finally feel that this is her home."

There's something about common experience that forms a bond between people, and parents and children in a stepfamily are no different. Anything that can isolate the stepfamily, that can screen out the distractions of an all-too-present world will work toward family cohesiveness. The sharing of jobs, discoveries, even disasters will bring a stepfamily together. Two families, both living in the Northwest, said that their love of the outdoors and their weekend camping trips provide the best melting pot around. One stepmother related, "We have all the camping gear for my little stepson. He lives in the city, so this is a novel experience for him, but it has really brought the family together. He's involved in almost every trip we take, and it makes him feel he's a part of us."

One stepfather said, "It has been hard for my own children to be a part of my new family because I live with my stepchildren. My own children, in effect, become visitors in my home. But planning some camping trips broke the ice, and we became a cooperative family unit. Since I'm part of a big family, I brought my stepchildren into it, too. My own kids made sure everyone knew they were all brothers and sisters, and I explained to my stepchildren that my children and my other relatives are all part of our family now, and each person should be treated accordingly. I'm glad to say my stepchildren responded beautifully."

Grandparents can be a great help in making stepchildren feel that they are a part of the family. But it's most important to recognize that if these are your parents, their first allegiance will be to you, and if you, as a stepparent, let your frustrations or momentary distaste or disaffection with your stepchild rub off on them, don't be surprised if they shun, or at most barely tolerate, your stepchildren. Beyond a sympathetic discussion of your stepchild's problems or habits, let the two generations work out their own relationship. But encourage your parents to help you out. They can give life to family history, they can widen your stepchild's acquaintanceship with other members of the family, they can provide another dimension of advice or assistance.

Derived from the recollections of children and their parents and stepparents, here are a number of things you can do to help children feel that they are a part of the family:

- Set up savings accounts for all the children in the same bank as yours.
- Whether they visit or live with you, keep their clothing and their sporting equipment on hand and accessible.
- Invite steprelatives around during visitation.
- Have specially prepared napkin rings or other personalized household items for each child.
- If they like a special glass or dish, keep it for their use only.
- Encourage each child to make something personal for another child's birthday or special occasion.
- Keep photographs of the children visible about the house.
- If you have a special skill—cooking, sewing, woodworking, athletics—go out of your way to teach it to your stepchild.
- When planning vacations, make sure each child has an equal say in where the family will go.
- Offer your stepchild something personal from your family—a bit of furniture, china, perhaps a collection, something that will strengthen the bond between you.

Helping your stepchild feel a part of your home and your life will give him fertile soil for putting down firmer roots. Your stepchild will remember you far more kindly than you expect. They told us so themselves. If we happen not to come up to par, they forgive, but when we go the extra mile, they are comforted.

Bibliography

Baer, Jean. *The Second Wife*. New York: Doubleday and Co., 1972.

Baruch, Dorothy W. and Miller, Hyman. *Sex in Marriage*. New York: Harper and Brothers, 1962.

Berkowitz, Bernard. "Legal Incidents of Today's 'Step' Relationship: 'Cinderella' Revisited." *Family Law Quarterly*, September 1970. 4:209–229.

Bernard, Jesse. *Remarriage, A Study of Marriage*. New York: Dryden Press, 1956.

Biller, Henry, and Meredith, Dennis. *Father Power*. New York: David McKay & Co., Inc., 1974.

Blaine, Graham B., Jr. "The Children of Divorce." *Atlantic Monthly*, March 1963. 211:98–101.

Blum, S. "Making Marriage Work: What Women and Men Learn from Past Mistakes." *Redbook Magazine*, February 1972. 138:84–85.

Bohannon, Paul, ed. *Divorce and After*. New York: Anchor Books, 1971.

Bowerman, Charles E., and Irish, Donald P. "Some Relationships of Stepchildren to Their Parents." *Marriage and Family Living*, May 1962. 24:113–21.

Brothers, Joyce. "Making a Second Marriage Work." *Good Housekeeping Magazine*, February 1972. 174:6.

Burchinal, Lee G. "Characteristics of Adolescents from Unbroken, Broken and Reconstituted Families." *Marriage and Family Living*, February 1964. 26:44–51.

Despert, J. Louise. *Children of Divorce*. New York: Doubleday and Company, 1953.

Disney, D. C. "Second Marriage—The Daughters Couldn't Get Along." *Ladies Home Journal*, August 1967. 84:18–22.

Duberman, Lucille. *Marriage and Its Alternatives*. New York, New York: Praeger Publishers, 1974.

———. *Reconstituted Family: A Study of Remarried Couples and Their Children*. New York: Nelson-Hall, 1975.

———. "Stepkin Relationships." *Journal of Marriage and the Family*, May 1973. 35:283–95.

Fast, Irene, and Cain, Albert. "The Stepparent Role—Potential for Disturbance in Family Functioning." *American Journal of Orthopsychiatry*, no. 36(1966):489–96.

Glick, Paul C., and Norton, Arthur J. "Perspectives on the Recent Upturn in Divorce and Remarriage." *Demography*, August 1973. 10:301–14.

Goldstein, Joseph; Solnit, Albert; and Freud, Anna. *Beyond the Best Interests of the Child.* New York: Free Press, 1973.

Krantzler, Mel. *Creative Divorce.* New York: M. Evans & Co., 1973.

Lowe, Patricia Tracey. *The Cruel Stepmother.* Englewood Cliffs, N.J.: Prentice-Hall, 1970.

Maddox, Brenda. *The Half-Parent.* New York: M. Evans and Co., 1975.

———. "Neither Witch Nor Good Fairy." *New York Times Sunday Magazine,* August 8, 1976. p. 16.

Noble, June and William. *The Custody Trap.* New York: Hawthorn Books, 1975.

Perry, Joseph B., and Pfuhl, Edwin H., Jr., "Adjustments of Children in 'Solo' and 'Remarriage' Homes." *Marriage and Family Living,* May 1963. 25:221–223.

Peterson, James. *Toward a Successful Marriage.* New York: Charles A. Scribners and Sons, 1960.

Podolsky, Edward. "The Emotional Problems of the Stepchild." *Mental Hygiene,* no. 39(1955):49–53.

Poussaint, A. A. "Are Second Marriages Better?" *Ebony Magazine,* March 1975. 30:55–56.

Roosevelt, Ruth, and Lofas, Jeannette. *Living in Step.* New York: Stein and Day, 1976.

Rydman, E. J. "Advice to Second Wives." *Harper's Bazaar,* April 1973. 106:104–105.

Salk, Lee. "You and Your Stepchildren." *Harper's Bazaar,* June 1975. 108:81.

Schulman, Gerda. "Myths That Intrude on the Adaptation of the Stepfamily." *Social Casework,* no. 53(1972):131–39.

Schwartz, Anne C. "Reflections on Divorce and Remarriage." *Social Casework,* no. 49(1968): 213–17.

Smith, William. *The Stepchild.* Chicago: University of Chicago Press, 1953.

Spock, Benjamin. *Problems of Parents.* Boston: Houghton Mifflin Co., 1962.

Stark, G. U. "Seven on a Honeymoon." *Parents Magazine,* May 1971. 46:445.

Stuart, Irving R., and Abt, Lawrence E., eds. *Children of Separation and Divorce.* New York: Grossman Publishers, 1972.

Tenenbaum, Samuel. *A Psychologist Looks at Marriage.* Cranbury, N.J.: A. S. Barnes & Co., 1968.

Thomson, Helen. *The Successful Stepparent.* New York: Harper and Row, 1966.

Index